Israeli Settlements on the West Bank

August 1977

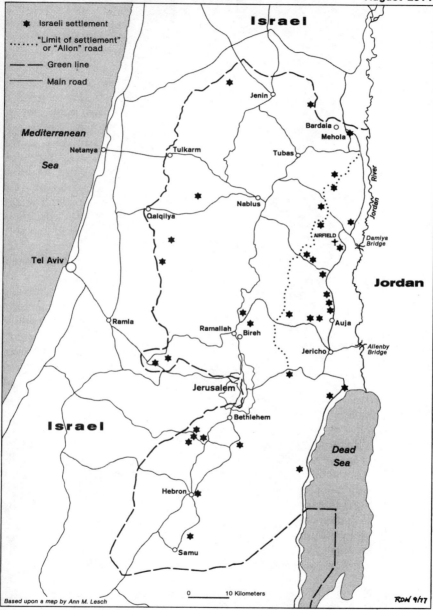

Legend:
- ✶ Israeli settlement
- ·········· "Limit of settlement" or "Allon" road
- — — Green line
- —— Main road

Israel

Mediterranean Sea

Jordan River

Jordan

Dead Sea

Israel

Locations labeled on map: Jenin, Bardaia, Mehola, Netanya, Tulkarm, Tubas, Nablus, Qalqilya, AIRFIELD, Damiya Bridge, Tel Aviv, Ramla, Ramallah, Bireh, Auja, Jericho, Allenby Bridge, Jerusalem, Bethlehem, Hebron, Samu

Based upon a map by Ann M. Lesch

Copyright 1977 by the Middle East Institute.

0   10 Kilometers

RDW 9/77

NOTE: Six suburban settlements and two industrial areas, all on the hills around Jerusalem, have been omitted from this map.

These are my Brothers

These are my Brothers

*Israel & the Occupied Territories
Part II*

Felicia Langer

Ithaca Press London 1979

CONTENTS

INTRODUCTION

Felicia Langer's book <u>With My Own Eyes</u> was first published in English
by Ithaca Press in 1975. Since then there have been more investigations
and reports. There can now be no doubt that Arabs have been tortured
by the Israeli authorities. There were Israelis - Felicia Langer among
them - who have been saying so for years. They were not believed.
The Israeli League for Human and Civil Rights, and its chairman Dr
Israel Shahak, published numerous reports especially concerned with the
Occupied Territories (those lands held by Israel since the June War of
1967, principally the West Bank and Gaza Strip). A number of the
League's documents were published in English as <u>The Shahak Papers</u>
(edited by Adnan Amad; NEEBII, Beirut).

Such evidence, though long disregarded both in Israel and in the West,
highlighted the pattern of oppression which characterized Israel's military administration of the Occupied Territories: the denial of human and
political rights; the arbitrary arrests and the sudden deportations; the
blowing-up of houses; the censorship and suppression of publications;
the seizure of Arab land for the establishment of (illegal) Jewish settlements in the area; and, most controversial of all, the torture and ill-
treatment of Arab prisoners.

It was this last which was hardest to prove, since what goes on in
Israeli prisons is for the most part a closely guarded secret. The
claims of Felicia Langer, Israel Shahak and others - that torture was
frequent and officially approved - were derided by the Israeli authorities.
Less easy to dismiss was the detailed report published on 19 June 1977
by the <u>Sunday Times</u> in London, whose six main conclusions may be
quoted:

'1   Israel's security and intelligence services ill-treat Arabs in
detention.

2   Some of the ill-treatment is merely primitive: prolonged
beatings, for example. But more refined techniques are also used,
including electric shock torture and confinement in specially con-
structed cells. This sort of apparatus, allied to the degree of organization evident in its application, removes Israel's practice from the
lesser realms of brutality and places it firmly in the category of
torture.

3   Torture takes place in at least six centres: at the prisons of
the four main occupied towns of Nablus, Ramallah and Hebron on the
West Bank, and Gaza in the South; at the detention centre in Jerusalem known as the Russian Compound; and at a special military
intelligence centre whose whereabouts are uncertain, but which
testimony suggests is somewhere inside the vast military supply base
at Sarafand, near Lod airport on the Jerusalem to Tel-Aviv road.
There is some evidence too that, at least for a time, there was a
second such camp somewhere near Gaza.

4   All of Israel's security services are implicated: the Shin Beth,
roughly Israel's MI5 and Special Branch in one, which reports to the
office of the Prime Minister; Military Intelligence, which reports to
the Minister of Defence; the border police and Latam, Israel's
Department for Special Missions, both of which report to the Police
Minister.

5   Torture is organized so methodically that it cannot be dismissed
as a handful of 'rogue cops' exceeding orders. It is systematic. It
appears to be sanctioned at some level as deliberate policy.

6   Torture seems to be used for three purposes. The first is, of
course, to extract information. The second motive, which seems at
least as common, is to induce people to confess to 'security' offences
of which they may, or may not, be guilty. The extracted confession
is then used as the principal evidence in court: Israel makes something of the fact that it has few political prisoners in its jails, only
those convicted according to law. The third purpose appears to be to
persuade Arabs in the Occupied Territories that it is least painful to
behave passively.'

The report, by the Insight team of the Sunday Times, gave careful
documentation of individual cases. Despite ritual denials, the Israeli
government has done nothing to refute the evidence put forward. This
report provides some of the most recent and most striking evidence of
repression in the Occupied Territories - evidence which is also given b

other sources.

Felicia Langer is a member of the Central Committee of the Israeli Communist Party - (Rakah) - and was recently elected as a Vice-President of the League of Human and Civil rights in Israel. She is a graduate of the Hebrew University Law School and is a member of the Israeli Bar. She has dedicated most of her professional life to the service of those who are in the most desperate need: Palestinian Arabs under Israeli rule. Through the cases documented in this volume (in which some parts of the Hebrew original were reduced) the reader will gain an insight into the reality of the post-1967 Israeli occupation and the quality of the Palestinian Arab resistance.

Allegations of torture in Israel hit the headlines again on 7 and 11 February 1979, when the <u>Washington Post</u> revealed the contents of various American State Department reports. One of these on human rights guardedly agreed that 'instances of mistreatment have occurred' and that the Geneva Convention has been ignored with expulsions, overcrowded prisons, administrative detention, illegal settlement and expropriations.

The first report, by Alexandra Johnson in May 1978 from the US Consulate in Jerusalem, gave detailed circumstantial evidence of forced confessions extracted by torture from fifteen people who became known to her through their application for US visas. The cable in November 1978 reported on another fourteen cases. Johnson's reports indicate that she gradually began to suspect that torture was a routine practice sanctioned by the Israeli military government on the West Bank and in Jerusalem. The men she interviewed spoke of similar instruments of turture in four different interrogation centres, suggesting 'standard issue equipment'. She also found indications of 'elaborate installation including hooks built into walls where suspects could be hung and beaten'. The <u>Post</u> articles aroused a storm of protest from Israel's supporters in the US, though the full contents of Johnson's cables are not yet published.

In this respect, the publication of the investigation under the title 'Israel and Torture' marks a historic breakthrough for the struggle against the violation of human, civil and political rights in the Occupied Territories under Israeli rule. In this victory Felicia Langer has an important share.

Felicia Langer, as many other Israelis is convinced, that a just peace between the Israeli and Palestinian peoples will be possible only after a total Israeli withdrawal from the occupied territories, the recognition of the legitimate rights of the Palestinian people, including its right to establish a sovereign state alongside Israel, and the right of the refugees to return to their homeland.

Felicia Langer has recorded events which must be placed within a context of continuing oppression. With remarkable dedication she continues to defend Arab prisoners under conditions which few lawyers, indeed few human beings, could endure; declaring to the world that 'these are my brothers'.

The Editors   March 1979
Ithaca Press
London

THESE ARE MY BROTHERS

Felicia Langer

THE BROTHERS

The car travels onward and I am absorbed in my thoughts. The passengers, two adults and the rest youths. The road leads to Nablus. The youths are discussing their studies and here and there an assessment of the post-October War political situation slips into the conversation. I try to listen, but my thoughts overwhelm me and I return to my own world.

I had hoped that the story of Hadija Abu Arkub and her torture would be among the last of my sad tales.[1] But it is not the case and again I am summoned to this painful subject.

The parents face me, their expressions full of fear and worry. They do not know the fate of their sons Bassem Amira and Wadji Kamhawi, both from Nablus, arrested at the beginning of 1974. They approached the League of Human Rights,[2] the Communist Party Knesset members, and then came to me for assistance.

I appeal to the Supreme Court and ask to see the youths

---

1. The book With My Own Eyes by Felicia Langer (Ithaca Press, London, 1975).
2. The parents met M Avi-Shaul, Deputy Chairperson, and he took care of their cases.

along with members of their families immediately. Of course
there is no "immediately", but my hope is that something will
begin to happen. Dr Hasin, Deputy-Attorney-General for the
State, says with fervor, "I have already been looking for Ms
Langer for several days." "I didn't know I was so difficult to
find," I reply. Nevertheless the order is given and it is possible
to visit the sons.

Bassem is detained in Hebron, Wadji in Jenin. In order
to appease the parents we must have sufficient time to visit them
both the same day.

The Amira family knows what it is to suffer. As the
father drives the car he speaks about one son now serving a
prison term in Nablus and about another who went to Jericho on
a trip with his class in 1968 and who has not been seen since.
Eyewitnesses said he was killed; some believe that the Israeli
Army was responsible. He was fifteen years old when he died.

The mother interrupts and points to the daughter, who
is listening intently to her father. "You know, she too feels the
occupation in her bones. Once she went to a demonstration with
other pupils and was badly beaten. Her whole body was black
and blue. I cried when I saw her. And the house ? That too
was destroyed."

I enter the Hebron prison. A dispute follows, as not
everyone understands the meaning of the order and the terms
of its text. "You are a lawyer, you see him, but what is this
about the family ?" I patiently explain the contents of the order,
which mentions the family. I notice the parents' faces and
understand that it will be terrible if they are not permitted to
see Bassem.

In the end, my interpretation is accepted and we enter
the prison hall. After a while Bassem is brought to us. His
expression shows both fear and joy. I have never seen him
before but the parents' suddenly gaping eyes of astonishment
chill my heart. He is thin. His head is shaven; his clothes
are dirty. He says in a trembling voice that if they had come

to see him earlier they would have noticed that he could not walk
at all. The investigators threw cold water on him, beat his entire body, and made him drink salt water. He was lubricated
with snow and they put a pole between his handcuffs and swung
him around in order to injure him. They succeeded. Bassem
showed me the scars and sores on his wrists. "They stripped
me nude during a snowy Hebron night and for about half an hour
I remained that way in the cell, barefoot, and afterwards I was
beaten again. My legs were swollen and I couldn't walk. I asked
for pity in the name of God, but they mocked me and said there
was no God here."

Bassem went on, and the parents listened. There were
tears in the father's eyes, the mother's were dry. I feverishly
recorded every word.

"They said I knew who tried to kill the Governor of
Nablus. They even tested me with a lie detector. I didn't do any-
thing and I told them that but they didn't believe me. I told them
I would die before I signed their lies," Bassem concluded.

We leave the prison without speaking and get into the
car. Wajdi's father asks, "How did it go ?" Everyone is quiet,
as a trip to Jenin to see his son still awaits us. Why should he
suffer further ? After a short while we sense the silence weigh-
ing us down and something explodes. Each of us, one by one,
speaks. Bassem's father says the least.

We approach Jenin. The hour is late. It is literally a
race against time. We feel the tension mounting in Wajdi's
parents. After a short while we enter the prison. Telephone
calls, questions, a few intentional delays in order to annoy us.
Some stinging remarks directed at me; I am left completely
indifferent. In this respect I have become immune. We are
taken to the prison office and Wajdi is brought to us from his
cell. His appearance is much better than Bassem's, but his
story is sad. "They slapped my face and spit in my mouth.
Afterwards, in some army prison they threw cold water on me,
made me drink salt water, and beat my entire body. They told me

it was my responsibility to confess my part in the attempt on the
Governor of Nablus's life. I told them I had alibis which could
be corroborated by one hundred Nablus merchants. It wasn't
enough for them."

We return and I draft letters of complaint to the Police
and Defence Ministers. It is certain that there is no evidence
against the two sons. I submit a request for bail to the Military
Court of Nablus.

On 19 February 1974 they are brought to court. I go
into the story of the tortures and ask the judge to look at Bassem's
wrists. The judge examines them and says, "Who knows where
this is from and how his hands looked before."

"There must have been an astonishing combination of
events for him to have injured both wrists in exactly the place
where his hands are now tied.....," I point out.

The officer in charge, encouraged by the judge's words,
says, "It looks like it is from the handcuffs when they aren't
closed well."

"Let's try an experiment during the break," I suggest.

The test is made. It does not confirm the officer's
claims. He smiles and remarks, "What's all the excitement
about ?"

Wajdi is freed on bail, but Bassem remains in prison.
No indictment was ever submitted. The Government issued an
administrative warrant for arrest, without charge or trial, and
he ramained in Nablus prison for more than a year. As for the
complaints to the Government, they succeeded no more than
others had over the years. The reply: "Such things never
happen."

Some time later, I was asked to take up the case of Bassem's
cousin Nabil Amira. His father, a grocer, sells his merchan-
dise from a cart and is regarded as one of the poorer residents
of Nablus. He is broken-hearted. His oldest son was imprisoned
in Nablus, released, and died soon afterwards. "He was always

healthy, " says the father. "He was a victim of imprisonment
and of your Occupation." His other son, Zouher, is now serving
a prison term. His third son, Nabil, is the sole breadwinner of
the family.

I visited him in Hebron at the beginning of March 1974.
He was brought to me from solitary confinement, pale and with
fresh scars on his chin. He began, "Now you come to me, after
such a long time, after they tortured me and nobody helped. Ask
the wardens how I looked. They are good people: they even tried
to help. They saw me wounded and bleeding." The two wardens
Nabil spoke about left the place in shock when they heard his
words. I asked one of them if Nabil was telling the truth about
his injuries. He answered in the affirmative but refrained from
further comment, claiming he did not know the source of the
wounds.

Nabil said that, immediately after his arrest, he was
brought to the Hebron Government Building and to its Investigation
Room. One of the investigators, named Johnny, began to slap
him and pull out his hair. Immediately, Nabil said, he felt
heavy dizziness, but that was only the beginning. Afterwards the
investigators stripped him and punched his entire body with their
fists.

One day he was brought to the Investigation Room, on
the window of which was set an iron pole hung with iron handcuffs.
His leg was put inside one of the handcuffs, his hands were
chained at the back and tied with rope. One of the investigators
pulled the rope, the second hit his legs. He showed me two black
toenails. The investigation continued for days and often into the
late hours of the night. The investigator (Johnny) said to Nabil
that just as Moses hit the rock with a stick and water flowed from
it, so after being beaten things would flow from Nabil's mouth,
information that the investigators wanted.

Once the investigators lifted up his legs and put them on
a chair. One of the investigators placed his foot on Nabil's
mouth and the second hit his legs with a stick. They made him

drink salt water without allowing him to spit, or vomit. They
laid him on the floor, forced his mouth open, and spat inside.
Then they forced him to swallow. Once they took him outside the
building during the night and poured cold water on him. He
screamed in the name of God, in the name of peace, but in vain.
This occurred several times during the night. When it snowed
he was taken outside, tied to a post, and left there. They also
put a stick in his anus and beat his sexual organs until he urinated
blood. Once they took him out at night and left him. He felt himself freezing completely. The investigators said they would torture
him until he died and afterwards would say he had committed
suicide, like Tashtush, the student from Nablus. They tugged at
him and he lost control of his frozen legs. He fell and lost consciousness. Nabil awoke in the Investigating Room with blood
all over him. He was carried back to jail and taken to the doctor.
The investigators ordered him to sign that the wound resulted
when he slipped and fell while looking for his shoe.... Only then
was he given medical attention, that is, a doctor was brought
to him and the cut was sewn up.

Still the torture did not end. He was slapped in the face
and the wound began to bleed. The investigators shaved his head
so that one could not see how much hair had been pulled from the
front of his scalp. The investigators also amused themselves
with Nabil. Once they tied a rope resembling a tail to his underwear, and commanded him to crawl on all fours and bark as they
threw pieces of bread into his mouth. "I was in solitary confinement for 85 days. Sometimes I thought I was going crazy and
that they were always coming to me to suggest suicide."

In the meantime Nabil was released. But a surprise
awaited his brother. After his imprisonment (a three-year sentence) an administrative order for his arrest was issued. The
Governor was not satisfied with the work of the military judges,
whom he himself had appointed, and so arrested Zouher about
twenty months after his sentence had been passed.

The father said to me, "Don't they have a God ?"

MAJDAL SHAMS

Majdal Shams is a village in a lovely mountainous area on the
slopes of Mount Hermon. Mount Hermon is called Jebel al-Shaikh
in Arabic, the mountain of the Shaikh, because the white blanket
covering it is like the Druze Shaikh's white head-covering.

The date is 7 March 1974. It is a normal day for the
Majdal Shams courts. Since the October War the military court
of the ghost town of Kuneitra, the one that dealt with those sons
of the mountain imprisoned in Israeli jails, has not been used.

The Mount Hermon roads are closed to private transport
today. Only those on official business may come and go. Since
the last war the tourists who enjoyed the waterfalls of the Banias
and the ski slopes of the Hermon have disappeared. The mountain
is once again a strictly military area. Inhabitants of the new
settlements, founded on the ruins of Syrian and Druze villages,
whose rightful dwellers now live in refugee camps near Damascus,
manage their "civilian" lives in bomb shelters.

Ten accused are being brought to court today. Hayil
Abu Jabal, Muhammad Maari, Rafik al-Halabi, Jamil Bathish,
Abdallah al-Kish, Asad al-Wili, Saliman Bathish, Salah Farhat,
Hani Zahwa and Hamed al-Kish. I represent seven of them. They
come from three villages on the mountain: Majdal Shams,
Masada and Bukata.

There is a crowd round the courthouse roadblock. I
have never seen so many although I have been "one of the family"
as an attorney in the Mount Hermon courts for over a year.
Hundreds of women and children are calling out the names of
prisoners. "If only I could look at them for a moment ! We
haven't seen their faces for months !" The detained have been
in prison for more than a year. A family visit, which means
that only two of the many family members are allowed at a time,
is permitted once a month.

One of the judges is late. The crowd gathers round the
doors. The little children are crying. Suddenly they discover
it is possible to "sneak in" at the windows and from there the

detained can be seen. They enter before the officers can manage
to prevent them. The police receive an order to disperse those
by the windows, but a few lucky ones succeed in exchanging a
smile and yelling a greeting. A hand opens the window from the
inside. Dozens of hands are extended in an attempt to touch the
prisoners.

I stand with the women who are outside the building. They
are mothers, grandmothers, sisters, and wives of prisoners.
They are not allowed to enter because there is not enough space.
Only one member of each family is permitted inside. Who will
be the lucky one among these masses ? "Hey, lawyer, take us,"
plead a few women. One of them says, "I'll carry your purse
and then I can go in, do me a favour !" Hayil Abu Jabal's grandmother attaches herself to me. Thin and small, she tries not to
be seen, but is discovered and pushed to the back. I hear her cry
"Felicia, let me see Hayil ! I haven't seen him for a year."

Trush Abu Jabal, Hayil's mother, enters. She is of
"privileged" family. Four of her sons are in prison. They have
already been sentenced. Hayil is the last remaining, and he will
receive his sentence today. The court begins late. The many
paragraphs of the indictment are read. They deal with spying
for the Syrian Intelligence; protesting against the occupation of
the Golan Heights and its annexation; armed infiltration;
possessing arms; and not reporting suspicious friends to the
police. The blame is attributed to Hamed al-Kish.

The accused plead innocent to the spying charge, but
confess to possessing arms and to   infiltration. It is
Hamed al-Kish who pleads guilty.

Among the detained are those who were severely
tortured during investigations, such as Hayil Abu Jabal, who
was sick as a result, Muhammad Maari, and Abdallah al-Kish.
Abdallah al-Kish suffered more than the others: he contracted
a serious lung disease as a result of particularly cruel treatment
during the investigation.

Everyone looks with admiration at Hayil Abu Jabal,

who is known for his pride.

Afternoon break. The accused eat with a few of their family and I am with them. They speak about the disengagement of forces, the long-awaited peace, and the end of the Occupation. "We'll invite you over, here or to Damascus, as you wish," they promise me.

All the detained, except Hamed al-Kish, whose trial will continue, have their trials postponed to allow the prosecution to prepare its case. They are taken from the auditorium to the police car. The audience that has crowded round the doors since the morning, unable to get in, still forms a solid wall round the building. The women scream, "Just let me touch them, just for a moment !" They pull at the prisoners' clothes as they are led to the car that is surrounded by policemen. Everywhere is chaos and crying. I stand among a crowd of women pushed from every direction. Maari's mother hugs me, "Felicia, please let me see him !" Maari is brought to the car without the mother and son even exchanging a glance. I calm the mother. At this moment I too am a mother. Cries are heard in the air, "Beloved, I am with you. It will be all right. You'll see !" From the side an angry curse is heard. A few policemen act humanely. The inhabitants are grateful. To one of the cruel ones they say, "Don't you have a father, or a sister, a mother or a brother ?"

Hamed al-Kish's trial continues. He is sentenced to three years. The part of the sentence which is unserved is suspended, and he is freed on the spot. The father's happy eyes give me the encouragement so necessary for me to continue....

Hamed sorrowfully leaves his friends who are returning to the jail where they have spent more than a year together.

Once in the car the prisoners say to me, "Do you understand how wrong those writers are, saying that we are a bunch of dissidents among the peaceful residents of the Golan Heights ? Did you see the crowd today ? We are part of the people and those who chatter about their desire to annex the area to Israel, they are the dissidents."

The car begins to move off. A few more of the family
have managed to see their dear ones for a few moments.

The long day is over.

MOTHER AND SONS

Her name is Trush Abu Jabal. She is like all mothers in the
world. She bore her sons in her home village of Majdal Shams,
at the foot of Mount Hermon. Two of them married and raised
families. Grandmother Trush loves her grandchildren like
grandmothers everywhere. What is more, they need special
attention because their fathers are not at home. For a year and
a half Aref and Adel have been imprisoned in far-away Ramla,
after being sentenced to long terms. In addition Trush is blessed
with two more sons. These two other sons, not yet married, are
also in prison. Fauzi and Hayil have had long sentences given them
by judges who sat in court and determined that they "threatened
the security of the area", referring to the (Syrian) Golan Heights.
Trush divides her time between visits to her sons in jail. Her
son Hayil, the most recently sentenced, said to her, "It won't
last long. Don't worry !" She accompanies him with her loving
glance as he is led from the court house to the police patrol and
back to jail again.

THE NATIONAL PALESTINIAN FRONT

On the eve of Independence Day, the Government of the occupation carried out mass arrests in the cities and villages of the West Bank and the Gaza Strip in a way unprecedented since the beginning of the Occupation. While the newspapers were told that these were "preventive" arrests, the Jerusalem police declared that it had found "extremists" and had discovered a hostile organization, The National Palestinian Front, set up - so the police claimed - by the Jordanian Communist Party. The papers reported more than forty arrests.

The newspaper al-Shaab - printed in Arab Jerusalem - reported that during the past Tuesday the police had issued administrative warrants of arrest for a period of three months against two youths, residents of the city, Yakoub Farah and Farouk Salfiti, who had been arrested several times during the Occupation.

It was announced also that among the arrested in Arab Jerusalem were the well-known journalist Ghassan Tahatub and a number of intellectuals and students. Also in Bethlehem, Beit Sahur, Ramallah, Jenin, Tul-Karem, and in Kalkilya members of the intelligentsia were arrested (engineers, teachers, doctors) together with workers, among them the Secretary of the Construction Workers Association in Ramallah, Adnan Dajar.,

It must be pointed out that the official Israeli media tried to justify these arbitrary arrests by presenting them as action against sedition, and by suggesting that these arrests were connected with the recent explosions in different parts of Israel and the Occupied Territories.

The media were also forced to announce that the latest police campaign was a sign of the Occupation Government's concern about the increasing political activities of the National Palestinian Front in the Occupied Territories. The Front had recently begun to print an illegal newspaper called Falestin, in which it was emphasized repeatedly that the main purposes of the Front were those that had appeared in the cover article of the first issue at the beginning of March 1974: "The struggle against the Occupation and the programmes of the Occupiers in the establishment of a civil administration. Struggle against all pro-imperialist forces that support these programmes. Resistance with force to the return of the West Bank to the Jordanian regime. The undermining of all schemes initiated by the reactionary Arab forces together with the imperialists. To take decisive action to achieve rights for our people, the Palestinians, for self-determination on its land under the leadership of the Palestinian National Front."

Among the arrested were Husni Hadad, an engineer from Bethlehem, whom I had known for years, the teacher Abed al-Majid Hamdan, and Atallah Rasmawi from Beit Sahu, a worker popular among the other workers. Their families came to me and I began my journeys to the prisons.

It became clear that the Shin Beit[1] was doing everything it could to stop me making any contact whatsoever with the prisoners, and trying to prevent me seeing them for even a moment. On 28 April I arrived at Hebron prison and after being granted permission to see Atallah Rasmawi and Abed al-Majid Hamdan, they told me they did not know what they had been arrested for, as they had not been interrogated at all. Suddenly a prison official appeared and ordered the meeting to stop immediately, claiming that: "You received them through an unfortunate error ! There is an order from the Deputy Governor of Hebron to forbid any visit to these prisoners. You can see them in another month." Afterwards it became clear that the detained men had received three-month administrative sentences.

The next day I went to the Ramallah jail to interview additional prisoners. Upon my arrival at the Registration Office I saw a man standing near the wall, facing it, and on his neck a white kafieh. Suddenly he turned his head and my blood froze: it was Suliman al-Najab, his eyes black as coal and his smile the smile of Suliman, whom I had not seen for about two years.

---

1. Israeli Intelligence

"Suliman", I cried out. "Felicia," he answered, and immediately
the Shin Beit surrounded us and it was then that I noticed the
presence of high-ranking officers and the extraordinary activity
going on in the prison.

They hustled me out of the room almost by force and
asked me to wait in the Director's Room, next to the Registration
Office. "Help yourself to biscuits and drinks, but please don't
leave," and they closed the door on me. I understood immediately that my seeing Suliman was for them an unpleasant "blunder"
and that they would try to prevent me speaking to him. The closed
door annoyed me and I asked them if I was being detained and if
so where the warrant for my arrest was. I left the room, moved
by a sense of danger for Suliman. "I must see him again," I
said to myself and approached the Registration Office. He was
still there and smiled, saying with emphasis on each word, "Tell
them about me at home." But at this point they again took me to
the Director's Room, and then I began to demand insistently that
I be given power of attorney over Suliman, but they would not
agree. I stayed in the room and peered through the small window
between the two rooms. Suliman saw me, but the prison official
closed the window immediately. Only afterwards did I understand
what a fateful meeting this was for Suliman and was grateful for
the chance that had brought me to Ramallah that same day.

I sensed it was necessary to get to work at once. I
submitted a request for an order nisi, which was granted on
7 May 1974, in which it was stated that it was up to the Ministers
of Defence and Police, "To come and explain why they continued
to forbid the petitioners and their attornies from coming to
interview the prisoners. "The next day I visited Ramallah prison
equipped with the order.

I requested an interview with some of my clients,
among them Suliman Najab, Adel al - Barguti, Mahmud Shikirat,
Ayid Nimar, Ghassan al-Harb, and others. Permission was
only given for some of the prisoners, in spite of the order nisi,
and the stubbornness of the Prison Director aroused my anxiety.

"I am afraid for them. Your stubbornness scares me because of
my bitter experience over the years. I agree not even to talk to
them. Just show them to me !" I said to the Director. He tried
to get clearance from the authorities(that is, the Shin Beit) but the
answer was negative. The Director tried to appease me by saying
"I promise you they are healthy and whole. With us there is no
torture, Madam."

The interviews with the "happy" prisoners began:
Communists, sent to prison for months, innocent. Among them are
those who have recently been put into prison and let out every few
months.

The last prisoner brought to me, whom I saw that day
for the first time, was young Ayid Nimar from the village of Ein
Arik near Ramallah. His face was covered with open wounds.
When I asked the source of these wounds the youth answered,
"Through torture. First of all, after I was arrested on 23 April
I met a member of the Red Cross. Afterwards they laid me on the
floor and kicked me in the face, causing the wounds which you see
now. Look at my hands too !" The prisoner showed me the signs
of injuries from the handcuffs on his hands, caused by the investigators putting extra pressure on them.

"The other prisoners witnessed my condition immediately
after the investigators did this to me."

"And what are you accused of ?"

"Belonging to the National Front in the West Bank."

I asked for the prisoner to have a medical check-up.
The wardens present said "We are not responsible for the investigation of Shin Beit people." I said to the Prison Director,
"I have witnessed with my own eyes the value of your assurance
that there is no torture here." My words were left unanswered.

HEBRON AND RAMALLAH

Nowadays the road to Hebron is not as it was in the past. It
reminds one of the stormy days of 1969 when the struggle against
the Occupation reached its height. At roadblocks, Israeli cars
pass without being checked, while Arabs are ordered to get out
of their cars and undergo a thorough check, including the car
itself. Someone expresses bitterness. His neighbour calms him
down. "If you talk so much they'll hold you for investigation
and then you will sit there till they free you." The second grumbles
"I had a work permit and now they have taken it away.
How will I survive ? They remembered that five years ago I was
detained...." Someone adds that King Hussein was no better.

The military court in Hebron is jammed with cases. It
is celebrating a "renaissance" since the relative quiet of the
period before the October War.

The tension is felt in Ramallah too. Near the prison wait
relatives of the prisoners. The jail, emptied before the October
War, has filled up again. The detainees are mostly Communists
arrested, supposedly, as preventive measures before Independence
Day. But this has been turned into three-month administrative
sentences. Many of them have been beaten, kept in solitary confinement, and nobody is allowed to see them.

Today in Military Court minor offences are being dis-
cussed: working in Israeli territory without a permit, harming
nature reserves, etc... A grown man stands before the judge:
"Why did you work without a permit ?" he asks. "Because they
don't give me a permit. What can I do ? All in all I worked one
day !" The judge takes pity on him and fines him forty Israeli
pounds or a week in prison . And so others too are convicted and
sentenced, learning the lesson that there must be order.

In front of the judge a youth with dark skin presents himself. His offence is of another sort. He took a small block of salt
from Ein Fasha on the Dead Sea shore. The site is a nature reserv
The prosecutor: "This is a serious offence. It is not necessary
to go into detail. We must educate people to respect nature res-

erves." The man does not understand. "I did not know at all that
it was forbidden. There wasn't even a sign," he says. The
judge: "If everyone acted like you, what would be left for us ?
I hope you won't do it again." "Of course I won't. If you say it's
forbidden, it's forbidden !" He is sentenced to a fine or imprisonment.

The families of the prisoners continue to wait outside the
jail. They await any news from the prisoners' attorneys. Perhaps
they succeed in seeing them. Worried faces. No good news.

Someone in the crowd asks quietly, "How long can it last ?"

LONDON-TEL AVIV 1974

London in May is like autumn, and it is difficult to sense the spring.
Between lectures, press interviews, and meetings with different
people, we talk with our friends. We speak of the fate of the area,
of the oppressed Palestinian people and how only the fulfilment of
their rights can bring the state of Israel full acceptance in the Middle
East: an Israel without dreams of expansion supported by the
Americans and existing at the expense of other peoples. I tell my
friends of those progressive Palestinians who seek to bring peace,
now rotting in prisons in Israel. I tell of my friends in Israel who
protest against the injustice, and before my eyes appears Ayid
Nimar and the open wounds on his face, and those whom I was not
permitted to see and whose fate I fear for. I turn to people of
conscience. My words ring. I hope they will reach the hearts
of people. It is only because I love my home and my people that
I am fearful and pained when in their name things are done that
should not be done.

At the beginning of June I returned to Israel after a

short visit to Paris. Far from the prisons, I thought about them
endlessly. It was as if they had become a part of me.

The Israeli sun demonstrated the graciousness of her
heart. The Shin Beit did not. They let me know immediately I
stepped from the plane that I was 'persona non grata' in my own
homeland.

But the difficulties were all still before me. When I got
back to work I understood at once that the torture machine was
now working full speed ahead. Walid Fahum (who was under
training in my office) following an appeal to the Supreme Court,
had seen Suliman al-Najab on 29 May 1974, in the presence of
the Shin Beit, and Suliman related what had happened to him.

He was arrested at five o'clock in the morning on
Tuesday 30 April in the Jordan Valley area. Two civilian vehicles
surrounded him; their passenges got out and he was dragged by
force into one of the cars. They blindfolded him, beat him,
screaming continuously, "Where have you been for the last four
years ?" They let out their four years of resentment.

Walid asked him, "How long were you interrogated ?"
He answered, "An eternity."

Walid asked, "What was revealed in the investigation ?"
He answered: "I have no information. I will answer all their
questions and investigations in court alone. The only thing I
have to tell them is my name, my identity number and my place
of birth - everything that is written on my birth certificate."

Suliman al-Najab revealed more: for fifteen days he
had not seen the light of day. His eyes had been covered the
entire time. His right leg was fastened to the iron door of his
prison cell by a chain thirty centimetres long. When he was
forced to stand he was attached to the door, and when he tried
to nap between tortures, he slept tied to the iron gate of the
dungeon. The investigation was accompanied by torture. He
was beaten in recurring patterns, mostly when he was naked.
In this way the blows could be more precise and effective. He
was beaten with a long thick stick; sometimes one leg was tied

to the floor while the other remained in the air.

He underwent the "falaka" torture. The person is seated on a chair, his arms and legs tied to it. The chair is then laid on the floor, and the soles of the feet beaten. The head is against the wall, so that with each blow on the feet the head strikes the wall. After the blows on his feet, he was forced to walk in the hall, pushed the whole time.

Likewise he was tied to a chair, naked, his hands handcuffed behind him. One of the team members would tread on the handcuffs with his whole weight; this would make him raise his entire body to ease the pressure on his hands. Then the other torturers would beat his sexual organs.

To Walid's question, "What kind of food did you get in prison ?", he answered, "I learned something from Nazim Hikmet[1]: that is, to start the food from the end. I ate in order to be able to stand in the investigations and torture. I hope you never in your life have to eat food like that. They served me a container in which there was some sort of mixture, a kind of dough of things which I could not separate."

On 17 May, Suliman al-Najab was transferred from Ramallah prison to the Detention House in West Jerusalem. He was brought there in a vehicle, blindfolded. Although he could see nothing, he knew that two other tortured prisoners were with him: Adel Barguti and Halil Hajazi. They were beaten during the entire journey and their heads knocked against each other. He never knew what happened to these two. Of himself he said that he too was beaten and tortured, and that he lost consciousness through the torture. He awoke when cold water was splashed on his face.

On 20 May the torture and investigation were stopped, and he was returned, after three days of torture, to the Ramallah prison. His legs continued to be tied. From 25 May he was removed from the cell and taken to the hall in the cell area.

---

1. Nazim Hikmet: the Turkish poet.

Here, too, his right leg was chained to a steel door.

To Walid's question, "What were you charged with ?" he answered, "They claim I am number one in the Jordanian Communist Party, that I am number two in the National Front in the West Bank, and number three in an armed organization, supposedly founded by these two organizations. I did not answer anything. During the torture I never opened my mouth. Eight years in al-Jafar jail in the Royal Hashemite Kingdom, from 1956 to 1965, strengthened and immunized me."

Suliman has a five-year-old daughter named Maha. When her aunt asked her where her daddy was, she answered, "Prison." "Why ?" she was asked, and she answered, "Because he loves his homeland."

Similar information was received from the lawyer Hanna Namara, whom I had asked to visit the prisoners while I was out of the country. He visited Nablus prison with the lawyer Ali Rafa, met the prisoners, and heard from them directly of the torture they were suffering. Their meetings in Nablus prison were on 2-4 June, and some of the prisoners already knew that worse was yet to come. The two lawyers met the following: Dr Farhan Abu Lail, Haldun Abed al-Hak, Latif Fahri Din, Rajah Ganayim, Rasan Hatib, Adel Zaga, Abed al-Baset al-Khayat, Muhammad Bagdadi, Ahmed Dahdul[1], Jamal Fretah, Muhammad Abd al-Hak and Halil Hajazi. Jamal, Muhammad and Halil complained that they had been tortured during their investigation.

Note: Ahmed Dahdul was killed on 22 March 1976 while in an army vehicle bringing him to the Tul Karem police station. In his wife's name I demanded to investigate, and the letter quoted below describes the tragic death:

"On 21 March 1976 the deceased was arrested by security forces in his home town of Salfit and was put into a car that was supposed to bring him to the Tul Karem police station. There were other prisoners with him in the vehicle, also residents of the town of Salfit. In this car the deceased was beaten severely by soldiers, in the presence of the other

prisoners. The car arrived at the Tul Karem police station
and the deceased was removed, showing no sign of life.
According to the official announcement, the deceased passed
away as the result of a heart attack.

"It was pointed out in evidence given by the doctor from Salfit
who had checked the deceased a number of times and knew him
well, Dr Mamduh Afana, that he had never suffered from heart
trouble. Furthermore, the deceased's wife and eyewitnesses
who saw him while he was being beaten by army personnel
blame the soldiers who beat him for causing his death.

"My client accuses the Governor of Tul Karem, as it was he
who commanded the soldiers to beat the deceased. She finds
support for this accusation in the fact that the Governor of
Tul Karem threatened the deceased, in the presence of his
sons, with arrest and deportation, and added that 'We have
another way...and that is before 22 March.' In order to
substantiate the accusation against the Military Governor of
Tul Karem my client brought evidence that on the road between
Nablus and Tul Karem, near the village of Anabta, the soldiers
who brought the deceased met the Governor of Tul Karm;
that they showed him the deceased and he replied, 'This is the
man .'

"The other prisoners who were in the car can testify to the
soldier's abuse of the deceased and they have evidence to
refute the argument that the deceased died a natural death.
In addition, there is no truth to the claim that the family of
the deceased refused to permit an autopsy. The truth is that
the family concurred in writing to the autopsy and it was
agreed that Dr M Afana would be present in the Legal Medical
Institute (The Pathological Institute) in Abu Kbir while it was
carried out.

"The deceased was a well-known public figure both inside
and outside his town. He was detained twelve years in a
Jordanian prison for being a Communist. During the Israeli

occupation he was detained approximately 21 months by administrative orders, and was freed from Nablus jail about two
months before his death. The deceased also submitted his
candidacy for the municipal elections in Salfit and according
to his wife's testimony the Military Governor was not pleased
with this.

"In the light of all the foregoing a most dismal picture is
painted of a criminal act against a powerless man, which
ended in his death during his imprisonment, when all responsibility falls on those who abused him and on their agents.

"Therefore, I request you to appoint an investigating committee
to inquire into the death, so that witnesses are heard and I myself can study the evidence and participate in the discussion
of the committee. Needless to say, those responsible for the
death must give account of their deeds so that the life of an
Arab prisoner will not be forgotten."

HALIL HAJAZI

Halil Hajazi is 38 years old and is the father of three children.
Since 22 April he has not been allowed to meet his family or see
a lawyer. Hajazi reported that the "investigators" beat him even
on the day of his arrest, in the Military Government building in
Nablus, with a stick on his sexual organs and other parts of his
body.

    For three days he was harshly tortured and when they
did not succeed in wringing the desired confession out of him,
the investigators transferred him to the Military Government
building in Ramallah.

    On his arrival there just before evening, he was

stripped, hung by his hands and beaten. The torture continued
the entire night. After a short break, it was renewed. Each
time he lost consciousness they would take him to the little
courtyard and pour cold water on him. The investigators threatened that they would kill him as they had killed Faris al-Tashtush
in the Nablus prison if he did not confess.

"There are four ways before you," they said to him.
"Three of them are in our hands: to kill you, to make you crazy
for the rest of your life, or to expel you to Jordan. The fourth
way is the simplest and it is in your hands - which is to confess."
Hajazi's answer was that he knew nothing and that there was
nothing for him to confess.

The torturers threatened to destroy his house and to turn
his wife into a prostitute.

Two days later the police appeared and ordered him to
get dressed to see his wife. They brought her - so they said -
to leave her with four soldiers so that they could do to her whatever they wished. When he entered the room, there sat his wife
next to a woman soldier. He asked to shake her hand, but the
police took him from the room immediately.

Afterwards Halil Hajazi was transferred from the
Ramallah prison by a border patrol car, his eyes blindfolded and
a sack over his head. Throughout the journey to Jerusalem
prison the border patrolmen never ceased to kick and beat him.

After twenty days of torture in Ramallah prison, during
which he was not allowed to wash his face even once, and then
further torture in the Jerusalem jail, Hajazi was returned to Nablus
prison, where new kinds of suffering were prepared for him.

He was brought into an extremely narrow room with a
floor of sharp portruding stones. Here he was forced to strip,
remove his shoes, and lie on the stones. The food served to him
was bread crumbs. In that same room he was forced to lift a
chair with tied hands and to stand on one foot while they beat him.
If he dared to lower his foot or drop the chair, they beat him
harder until he 'reformed'.

Muhammad Abbas al-Haq, 37 years old, the father of three children, who works as an engineer in the Nablus municipality, told the lawyers of the severe tortures he endured. His story is almost identical to the previous one. Sharp stones, beatings on the souls of his feet, the extinguishing of cigarettes on his skin. After a time, he is imprisoned in an extremely narrow cell. It is impossible to sleep in it, and his hands are tied.

His health deteriorated. His request for medical care was ignored.

The lawyer Nakara also saw Husni Hadad in Hebron prison during my absence from Israel. Husni as yet had no complaints. He also did not know that the difficult part was still before him. Atallah Rasmawi complained about his lungs, but he too could not imagine that what had happened up till then would serve only as a foretaste of what was to come.

We tried to alert public opinion. The League of Human Rights gave a press conference where, in addition to the lawyers, the League chairman, Professor Israel Shahak, and his Deputy, the author Avi Shaul, were present. The press came, listened, received a memorandum prepared by the League, and asked about private evidence: the next day nothing was written. The conspiracy of silence, so efficient a method, worked this time as well.

But it is impossible to keep everyone quiet. Rakah[1] representatives in the Knesset and Meir Vilner, the Secretary-General of the Party, sent urgent appeals to the Prime Minister. The Democratic Women's Movement appealed to the President over the arrests and torture. The Israeli women visited the wives of those detained in Nablus and Ramallah. The League of Human Rights launched a publicity campaign about the prisoners and their torture, and claimed that the arrests were detrimental to the state of Israel.

The newspaper of the Student Committee at the Hebrew

---

1. The Communist Party of Israel

University, 'Pi Ha-ton', gave wide publicity to the torture of
Suliman al-Najab.

SULIMAN

After my return I applied to see Suliman in prison. The game of
cat and mouse is the Shin Beit's favourite. I was told that Suliman
was in Ramallah prison, and when I went to that jail, I was told he
was not there. I threatened to submit an additional plea to the
Supreme Court, and then the Shin Beit agreed to let both me and
his wife see him, in Ramallah prison.

      Rukieh, his sister, Leila, his wife, the children and I
myself all arrived at the prison. The tension was almost unbearable. What we had heard of their torture shocked all of us and
the period in which he had disappeared again worried us greatly.
We sat in the waiting-room intended for family visits. It was
Friday and the room was full of visitors. Rukieh the beloved
sister, who resembles Suliman as two drops of water do, hoped
that they would agree to let her see him. Full of optimism and
love of life, Rukieh tried to encourage all of us, but it was hard
for her to conceal her own worry. I was called by a Shin Beit
official called Abu al-Abed who was responsible for the visit.
Suliman is brought into the Prison Director's room. His face is
yellow but there is a smile on his lips. This is the first visit
since I met him by chance on the day of his arrest, when I was
in Ramallah prison. Abu al-Abed's eyes are well known to me.
They pierce me like knives. I am excited and wish to tell Suliman
of the love of his friends, the respect of his people and something
from me. I am but an attorney for Suliman the Communist, who
has not broken any law in the world. Abu al-Abed's cold voice

returns me to reality.

"I warn you, if you don't limit yourself to a short conversation on legal defence matters I will stop the interview at once."

"How are you, Suliman ? Where have you been all this time ?"

"I was in Sarfand. They tortured me again. I was in a cell...."

Shin Beit official: "I'll stop the visit immediately."

"These questions are required precisely for the defence of this man to whom I have been appointed, and to which you have agreed."

Shin Beit official: "I don't want any details !"

Suliman: "Abu al-Abed did not beat me. But the others – it was terrible..."

He tried to show me the marks of his torture on his legs. He stoops to roll up his trousers.

Shin Beit official: "If you try to show anything I shall stop the visit. Hey, Suliman, isn't it true I treated you OK the whole time ?"

Suliman: "True, you really were OK with me."

Suliman: "You're optimistic, Felicia. Yes, so am I."

"What are you accused of ?" I ask.

"That I am a leader of the Jordanian Communist Party, a leader of the National Palestinian Front, that I was responsible for violent acts, etc...I denied everything and said I would speak in court. They said I wouldn't have a trial. After I met a lawyer from your office they took me to Sarfand and tortured me again. I don't know what will be done when you leave me today. I'm ready for anything."

I say to the Shin Beit officer, "You are responsible for every hair that falls from his head. I promise you that I won't hesitate to appeal to all appropriate institutions in Israel and throughout the world. During my last visit to London and Paris I found how concerned people were about the abuse of prisoners."

Suliman: "They can treat me as they like. The outcome will not change, and they know it. I have requested medical care. I am sick, and have as yet received no treatment."

At this moment, the Director of Ramallah prison entered. I turned to him and demanded medical attention for Suliman. The Director said, "He should go to the medic." "I look to you in the presence of witnesses and place full responsibility on you for Suliman's health." I told Suliman, "The Communist Knesset members won't hesitate to do anything for you, out of solidarity for people like you..."

Shin Beit official: "Is that all ?"

Suliman to the official: "I am a political prisoner and therefore I would like to request that my lawyer give me a report on the latest political events."

Shin Beit official: "No, that's forbidden. I will tell you everything. After all, we've spoken already about both politics and poetry."

Suliman: "Maybe Felicia could also be present in a meeting with my wife."

Shin Beit official: "No, that's forbidden."

Suliman (to me): "I thank you all very very much. Yours is the other face of your people. Thanks to you we can believe that peace will come."

I reply, "Don't thank me for what must be done. You see that we couldn't prevent your torture up till now. We hope to prevent it from now on."

Suliman: "Goodbye until we meet again."

The farewell was difficult for me and with a heavy heart I left him, feeling how much he wanted to talk and could not.

The fate of Suliman aroused fear in us for the fate of the others. I tried to locate the places of detention of Halil Hajazi, Jamal Fretah, Adel Barguti, Husni Hadad, Atallah Rasmawi, Ghassan al-Harb, Abdallah al-Beraat and Muhammad Abu Garbieh. In the meantime Suliman disappeared from Ramallah prison. The others I was not allowed to see, the Shin Beit again playing cat and mouse. The mothers, wives and sisters became an almost integral part of the office, which became a headquarters for the search for their dear ones, my clerk Yona and Walid devotedly helping me. After about ten days of postponements and manoeuvres I decided to appeal again to the Supreme Court, to protest at the disappearances and tell of the fears of their relatives (especially since the meeting with Suliman) that they were being tortured.

At the same time, Rakah members of the Knesset sent a memorandum to the Prime Minister and the Minister of Justice in which they demanded the immediate cessation of torture of the prisoners and their early release. All the families of the prisoners appealed to the Israeli public in a proclamation sent to the Press and to democratic circles in Israel:

"We appeal to you in this proclamation, two months after the arrest of our relatives, beginning on 22 April 1974, in the hope that the memory of millions of Jewish victims of barbaric Nazism has instilled in many of you an abhorrence of all in-justice.

"Our brothers, fathers and husbands were detained as 'preventive arrests' according to the Military Government Authorities, on the eve of the Israeli holiday and they are still detained in prison, while no blame is attached to most of them. Some of them, according to what we have been told by their lawyers, have been tortured, and are still subject to abhorrent physical and mental suffering.

"The fact that we have been prevented from visiting them, although the legal investigation period is now over, arouses fear. The authorities still withhold the whereabouts of the prisoners Suliman Najab, Muhammad Abu Garbieh, Abdalla Beraat, Husni Hadad and others.

"The Military Authorities try to justify their arbitrary behaviour to the Israeli public by claiming that these prisoners established a terrorist organization. The authorities use this all-inclusive term with no explanation.

"But the truth is, as the Military Authorities know, as do

democratic people in Israel, that they are supporters of a just
peace, struggling constantly against reaction wherever it is
found. They firmly support the solution of the Middle East
conflict on the basis of international decisions and the honouring
of the rights of all peoples of the area to live within secure
borders, including the people of Israel and the Palestinian Arab
people.

"The arrests, the torture, the prohibition of our visiting them
and the concealment of their places of detention do not serve
peacemaking and are contrary to the true aspirations of our
people and to internationally recognized human rights.

"We appeal to all people who want a just victory, intelligence
and realism to be part of the solution of the Arab-Israeli conflict, to those who are supporters of democratic principles and
justice without distinction of race or colour. We ask them to
demonstrate solidarity with us, and to protest at the continued
detention and torture of our relatives and to demand their
immediate release."

Information on their arrests appeared in the foreign press
in Europe and the USA. Eighty-three political and student organizations in the USSR appealed to the UN in protest at the arrests
in the West Bank. Public figures such as Daniel Amit and Natan
Yelin Mor raised their voices against the arrests.

JUDGEMENT DAY

The day of the hearing of the plea, 2 July 1974, arrived. The hall
was packed with the prisoners' families. The judges are Sussman,
Vitkin and Asher. Well-informed sources say that it is not good.
Before I open my mouth the State attorney, Dr Hasin, begins,

and his voice thunders, "Ms Langer has a xerox machine and she
submits pleas as if they were nothing. And she accompanies them
with loud publicity claiming that the prisoners are being tortured."
I try to protest at his words and show that no-one answers and nobody responds to my appeals seriously. Meanwhile the families
are terrified, especially after what happened to Suliman when he
was not permitted to show me his wounds.

Dr Hasin jumps from his seat and roars, "She wanted
Suliman to do a 'strip-tease' in the middle of Ramallah prison.
Of course it was not allowed." The blood rises to my head and I
reply, "Will this shameful and audacious attack never stop ?"
The judges calm down the learned doctor who has lost his temper
in defence of Shin Beit personnel. I speak about basic human
rights, of disrespect for human dignity. The judges question Dr
Hasin: President S Sussman agrees that there has been disregard
for human rights here. Dr Hasin says that of course there is
nothing to prevent me from seeing all the prisoners, and I agree
to cancel the plea. It is close to two o'clock and I arrange my
visit to Jalame for the same day, to see Suliman, Halil Hajazi,
Gamal Fretah, Ghassan Harb and Muhammad Abu Garbieh. The
visit to Hebron is set for the next day.

The car advances, carrying the members of the family and myself. That we won't be late, that they won't say to us that today
is impossible.... Rikieh is with us too. Permission to visit is
for me alone but at least she will be close to the place where
Suliman is held.

We arrive at Jalame prison. Outside is a pastoral view
with green trees, peace and quiet. Among the trees stand the walls
of the prison. The Director arranges that the visit will take place
in the solitary confinement wing. I enter the building by way of the
steel gate. On one of the doors is a sign that says 'Out of Bounds'.
The whole place is desolate. A few abandoned rooms along the
hallway. Dead silence. How strange when one compares it to
the roar of the back part of the jail.

The man who will supervise the visit is a Shin Beit official called Abu Nabil, a well-mannered man; they have never complained of him beating them. "His role is to be the 'good investigator'", prisoners told me more than once. "He's the one who
comes to you after the others have already beaten you sufficiently
and he 'saves' you from them, provided of course that you talk..."
       We are in a large room with only a table in it. Abu Nabil
sits down across from me. First Suliman is brought to me. I am
stunned by the look of his face, his dull eyes and the unnatural way
his head bends over. Saddest of all was his smile, which did not
brighten his eyes at all. I asked him to tell me everything and he
said to me, 'I will tell you what Abu al-Abed forbade me to tell
you then, in our meeting in Ramallah." I recorded his story as
Abu Nabil listened to every word:
       "On 4 June I was taken to a military jail at Sarfand,
apparently. The next day I was brought to the office, tied, and they
began to hit me. Beatings of this sort continued for three days.
Afterwards I was taken to a solitary cell about 50 cm by 50 cm
in area and 1.60 metres in height. The floor was strewn with
sharp stones. Every movement I made hurt me. I was as naked
as the day I was born. I was taken from there by soldiers, who
put a sack over my head, to the courtyard and forced to crawl on
all fours. When I crawled slowly they beat me. When all the
skin had been scraped off my knees from the rubbing I refused to
continue. The soldiers beat me again. I hid my head on the
ground. I was taken back to the cell. Then I was forced to carry
a chair in my arms. I was in the cell for about forty-eight hours
and was ordered to carry the chair every so often. Then I was
taken back to Ramallah prison, and was there until 14 June 1974,
the day you saw me. The marks from the wounds on my legs
were still fresh, and therefore Abu al-Abed didn't allow me to
show them to you."

At this point Suliman rolled his trousers up over his knee. I
saw clearly that the layer of skin on his knees was new. He poin-

ted out that it was in exactly those placed that the skin rubbed off as a result of the crawling. Suliman continued, "During your visit to me I expressed the fear that I would return to the torture, and that is what happened. The same day, at 5 o'clock in the afternoon, I was taken from Ramallah to the military prison, and there again put in a small cell, which I have already described. I remained there until Sunday and on the same day I was brought to the prison office and beaten all over, including my sexual organs. My interrogators sprayed my testicles with a strong chemical which began to hurt very much, as if they were burning. They also sprayed the nipples on my chest."

Suliman showed me his chest and I saw for myself that the top layer of skin near the nipples had peeled off, and that the skin was very red, and new, as if grown after burns.

Suliman continued, "Then I was again taken to the cell until 21 June, and again sprayed with the same chemical. I was also hung by my arms on the grill of the window. The torture went on until 28 June, the day I was taken here, where you now see me. I am now in a cell whose only window is closed. When I said I had no air to breathe, they said I was going to die anyway."

I wrote, my hands trembling, and when Suliman showed me his chest, with the raw nipples, Abu Nabil saw it too. I said to him "Remember well what you have heard and seen now - the day will come when you will be called to testify to it."

The second man to enter the room was Halil Hajazi. I saw him for the first time. He walked with difficulty, with his legs spread apart. (Afterwards he told me that the burning in his testicles caused him terrible pain and made walking difficult). When he saw my reaction to his walking he tried to smile at me, and I became aware of the unusual sense of humour of this tortured man. I asked him to tell me everything and he began, "I was beaten and tortured after my arrest, and I reported this to my lawyers Hanna Nikara and Ali Rafa, who visited my on 4 June 1974 or so in Nablus prison. After their visit I was taken to the military prison and beaten on my head till it bled.   They brought me a medic to treat it. My hands were tied behind me. My legs were beaten with sticks."

In the presence of Abu Nabil, Halil showed me the soles of his feet. I saw skin peeling off in the middle and black marks near the toes. In addition, I saw wounds forming scabs near both ankles. Halil explained that he had been handcuffed, and that the investigators had pressed on them until they hurt. He continued, "For ten days I couldn't walk at all. As a result of the pain in my jaws from the investigators' blows, I couldn't eat either. The man facing us (Abu Nabil) acted humanely towards me. He even asked my torturers to stop. The investigators also beat my testicles and sprayed me with chemicals. The Shin Beit people would bring soldiers to see how I was tortured. My testicles swelled after the spraying and I needed medical attention, and asked for it."

In this instance as well I appealed to Abu Nabil, so that he would see Halil's legs. Never had I felt such anger. But Halil's spirit was high despite the wounds and the pain. He told me and Abu Nabil, "When I talked about peace and the possibilities of co-existence, they beat me more. Did that annoy them so much ?"

The third man was Jamal Fretah. The black mark of a blow under his left eye was evidence of the treatment he had undergone. He appeared very weak and spoke with difficulty. He told me that about forty days before, after he had met my trainee Walid Fahum, he had been taken to military jail. There he was forced to lie on a floor paved with sharp stones, stripped naked. He suffered knee injuries from this, and showed me the scars from the rubbing on his left knee. I remarked on the black mark under his eye. He told me it was from the blows he had received on his face, and that because of them he was having difficulty in hearing well. He told me that he had remained tied for twenty days, and that afterwards his hands were almost paralysed, and still hurt him even today. He said that he had seen the sun today for the first time in forty days, when he came to meet me.

Ghassan al-Harb's situation was no better. He too I met for the first time. He appeared weak and exhausted, and told me that on 11 June 1974 he had been taken from Ramallah prison to a military jail. There he had been put in a small cell with a floor scattered with stones. His investigators had stripped him naked, put a sack over his head and dragged him over the rough floor of the cell. He showed me scars on his right hand. The interrogators, or others, he had not seen, laid on top of him and one of them struck his head on something hard on the floor. His torture went on for only one day, a short period compared to that of his friends.

The last was Muhammad Abu Garbieh. His situation was somewhat better than that of the others. He was nevertheless taken to military prison and beaten, but when he said that his son was ill with tuberculosis, and his interrogators were convinced that there was truth in his words, they stopped beating him.

The meeting ended and I had to leave and speak to the families, and calm them down. I knew that my face would betray me and that I could not hide the truth, and so it was. I hope they forgave me for my weakness.

Leila Najab and Afaf al-Harb fought for their husbands. They appeared at public meetings and protested at the detention of the others. Afaf al-Harb's personality kindled the confidence of the other women. She worked for her husband during the last days of her pregnancy, which took place at the most difficult time of her life. Leila Najab appeared a number of times before Israeli audiences and spoke to their hearts and consciences: all who heard her were impressed by the force of her sincerity.

The rest of the women also took part in the struggle to free their dear ones: Abdallah al-Beraat's wife, the mother of Halil Toma, the well-known poet, Yakoub Farah's mother, Muhammad and Hussein Abu Garbieh's mother, and many others. They deeply impressed all who came into contact with them.

HUSNI AND ATALLAH

I now saw Husni Hadad, an engineer from Bethlehem and an old
aquaintance, in Hebron prison, two days after my visit to Jalame,
for the first time since his arrest. The first thing which struck
me was his thinness. When I arrived he was sitting with a representative of the Red Cross, and showing the marks of cigarettes
that had been extinguished on his legs. When I shook his hand I
looked at his red eyes and saw that he had aged suddenly many
years.

On 26 May 1974 or thereabouts he was taken to the
military jail. His clothes were taken from him and he was dressed
in military garb. For thirty-two days he was detained there,
except for two days when he was in Jerusalem Detention House.
There he met his family. For the entire time in military prison
Husni's hands were tied and he was barefoot. Whenever the
investigators took him out of his cell they put a black bag over
his head. About the end of May Husni, after being taken from his
cell to the courtyard, was forced to crawl on his knees with his
hands tied above his head. This went on three times a day for
two days, after every meal. He was also forced to hold a chair
while standing on one leg, and to walk down a very narrow ditch
with a bag over his head, constantly falling. Periodically he was
forced to jump into this ditch. He found difficulty in breathing,
as not enough air came into the sack, but when he slowed down
they beat him. Suddenly he felt someone sit on his arms. After
he had several times refused to crawl, he was badly beaten all
over, including his eyes, and one of his ribs was broken. He
continued to crawl in spite of his knees being cut and bleeding.

Between torture, he was taken to one of the dungeons,
the worst of which was 75 cm square and 160 cm in height with
a floor covered with stones. His arms were tied from behind
so that he could get no sleep.

According to Husni's description, food portions were
literally starvation rations. There was no cooked food. During

thirty-two days he lost ten kg. The lavatory was in the same cell
as himself. There was no opportunity to wash. Liquids were
rare - sometimes Husni went a full day without water. During
the same period he saw Atallah Rasmawi, Halil Hajazi, Muhammad
Abbas al-Haq and Jamal Fretah in that same prison. He heard the
screams of the latter for hours. The investigators extinguished
cigarettes on his legs and Husni showed me signs of this. Likewise
the investigators threatened him that he would be sent to a concen-
tration camp in Sinai.

Atallah Rasmawi[1], the solidly built labourer, looks pale
as a ghost. The story of his torture is almost identical with that
of Husni except for the march in the narrow ditch. His torture,
however, lasted much longer, and once he was beaten with such
ferocity that he thought the end had come. He showed me loose
black toenails which resulted from the beatings. Eating and
sanitary conditions were similar to Husni's. He was being investigated without charge just like Husni and the rest of the prisoners
in Jalame and the other prisons,about his connection with the Jordanian Communist Party and the National Palestinian Front.

---

1.   On 12 April 1976 municipal elections were held in the West
Bank. They were marked by forceful opposition on the part of
West Bank residents to the so-called 'self-rule' suggested by
the Israeli Government. This was designed to perpetuate the
occupation and promote a leadership to compete with the PLO
while all the patriotic forces in the West Bank repeatedly stressed
that their only representative was the Palestine Liberation
Organization.

At the height of the elections, the Israeli Government
took a step which symbolized its involvement in the elections.
On April 27 Dr Ahmad Hamzeh al-Natsha of Hebron, Director of
the government hospital in Bethlehem, and Dr Hadj Ahmad of
al-Bira, a well-known dentist active in the Dentists' Union, were
deported to Lebanon. Both were well-known progressives and
candidates for the elections and it was apparent that Dr al-Natsha's

chances of election as Mayor of Hebron, in place of the Israeli
Government favourite Sheikh Muhammad Ali al-Jabari, were good.
The expulsion was carried out fifteen minutes before his appeal
to the Supreme Court which I had submitted in the name of his
wife Louisette on Saturday, and which was heard in the judge's
home. The way in which the expulsions were carried out, which
constituted an unprecedented contempt of court, aroused so much
resentment on the part of Judge Etzioni, who was judge on that day,
that he expressed it in his decision. The expulsion and its arbitrary
manner aroused sharp criticism in many circles in Israel, including several Government officials, as well as in the world press.

Several moments before the closing of the list of candidates, we succeeding in submitting the candidacy of
Atallah Rasmawi, held in administrative detention, after signing
him the necessary documents in Hebron prison with the help of a
local lawyer, Ziad Jasar, and with the approval of the Attorney
General of the West Bank.

On election day 1, 318 voters cast their ballots for
Atallah Rasmawi and he was fourth among eight members of the
council. We immediately began to work for his release from
prison. The municipal council of Bet Sahur announced that it
would not assemble until Atallah Rasmawi was one of its members.

In Nablus, Haldun Abd al-Haq, who several months
previously had been released from jail, was elected.

All over the West Bank candidates from the patriotic and
nationalists were chosen, and this was seen as a defeat for the
official Israeli outlook and a demonstration against the occupation,
and this without any terror or oppression.

HALDUN ABD AL-HAQ

His name is Bakr Abd al-Haq. He is four years old. Together with his older sister and brother, he was visiting his father, Haldun Abd al-Haq, in Yagur (Jamale) prison.

A pastoral view with green tree-tops and mountains. We are in the abandoned courtyard. There is junk in every corner. Are there any people here ? There is not a voice, not a whisper, nor any other clue of human presence....This is the dungeon wing, the solitary confinement cells, and thus the silence is explained. Who can the prisoner speak to when he is by himself the entire day and does not even have a daily outing ?

Haldun Abd al-Haq hugs his son. The boy asks the difficult question, "Daddy, when will they let you come home ?" The father answers with a smile on his lips, "I don't know." The boy looks around and repeats his question. The father doesn't answer. The mother looks at the Shin Beit man present at the meeting. His face is dulled.

Haldun says, "They took me to some place in the military prison, so they told me. There they stripped me. I protested. I told them it was awful to strip a grown man, and to leave him that way. A soldier came and hit me hard on my neck. I was hung by both hands. I stayed like that for a long time. Then they took me down and I was led to a dungeon, its floor strewn with stones, and from there to a small cell 60 by 60 cm and 1.60 metres high. It was impossible to stand there and impossible to sleep."

Young Bakr did not understand. His brother did. His eyes are wild. Bakr saves the situation, "Daddy, I brought you some dates." He takes a few dates from the paper in which they are wrapped and gives them to his father. "This is from our tree" he says proudly. The father eats them with enjoyment. The wife sits across from him and is silent. It appears that she will soon give birth. "We'll call the baby Faraj" (Release). She smiles for the first time during the visit. After fifteen minutes the guard declares, "The visit is over."

My second visit with Haldun takes place in the prison

office in the presence of Abu Nabil. Haldun, who is still in the
dungeon, jokes around, and his unusual humour in these conditions
warms my heart. He speaks of Palestinian rights and how Israel
must recognize them. Haldun Abd al-Haq was imprisoned for
nearly two years. During my visits I saw his strength, a smile
and joke always with him.

ABU AHMAD (FATHER OF AHMAD)

He is about fifty-six years old and his name is Muhammad Atwal.
Today I know his son, Ahmad, a student of international relations
at Kiev University, his mother, and his young blue-eyed brother.
    When I saw him in the dark room in the 'Russian Com-
pound' I thought only of how to prevent his suffering. Afterwards
it became clear that I had not succeeded, at least not during the
period in prison nor after his release. Abu Ahmad was released
at the end of thirty days in prison, without a charge made against
him. Frail, with a pale face and soft speech, he told me that he
had been badly beaten during the investigation on 8 May 1974 in
the Russian Compound prison.
    After his release he was again summoned to the invest-
igation office at Jerusalem police station, and the next day he
came to my office. His face was yellow and his hands trembling.
Here is his story: When he arrived at the investigation office on
2 June, four investigators surrounded him and beat his entire
body, concentrating on his sexual organs and the back of his neck.
They forced him to hold up a chair for a quarter of an hour,
threatening that if he lowered it they would beat him about the
head with it. He fainted, and when he came round he was pushed
out into the street, having been given a summons to appear for

investigation the following morning, and being told several times
that he should co-operate with them.

In fear for his life, Atwal refused to go to the investigation
alone. He asked me to accompany him. On 3 June I went with him,
along with Walid Fahum, to the department of investigations at
Jerusalem police station. I explained to the responsible official
that the man feared more injuries, and that the investigators would
be held responsible for any injuries which might endanger his life.
The official promised to take care of the matter. When he saw
Atwal's situation he showed understanding.

The next day Atwal came to my office, his legs weak,
and with another summons to the police station for that same
morning.

Suddenly he felt ill. My secretary, Yona Salman, asked
if he needed help, and he answered that his testicles and sexual
organ were bleeding as a result of the beating received at the
police station, already described to us.

After a doctor had examined him he was sent to the
Hospice Hospital in East Jerusalem. Representatives of the Red
Cross visited him in hospital on 5 June 1974.

Afterwards Atwal saw an official of Amnesty International
and gave her his bloodstained underpants as evidence. Up until
now Amnesty has published nothing of his abuse. More recently
at the beginning of 1976, Atwal met Eric Silver of the London
Observer accompanied, at his request, by an interpreter, the
journalist Rejwan.

The same correspondent sought me out in connection with
the torture of another of my clients, Shouki Hatib. I told him that
his newspaper had not printed the interview I had had with him in
London in October of this same year, even though I was described
as reliable and sincere by the interviewer. Instead an article by
Colin Legum had appeared, claiming that there is no torture
during investigations in Israel, that everything is fine, and that
I simply distort the facts. I wrote a letter to the newspaper in
response; and to Mr Silver I said I was ready to discuss the

topic with him. Then he made the well-known claim, "We need
hard evidence when it comes to matters of torture. Otherwise it
is impossible to print." I told him that they, the English, have
double standards towards the quality of evidence needed to
arouse suspicion of torture. At about this time the British
Dr Cassidy arrived from Chile claiming that she had been harshly
tortured there. Her evidence was at once accepted as reliable,
even though she had no 'hard evidence'. But from the Palestinians
hard evidence is demanded. "What do you expect, that the Shin
Beit official will admit now that he beat and tortured ?" Mr
Silver answered that justice is with me (maybe !), and then I
suggested that he interviewed Atwal, the only victim of torture
who, at that time, was not in jail. On the appointed day Atwal
came to my office. It was shortly after the operation on his
sexual organs as a result of 'treatment' during investigations.
He talked to Mr Silver for a long time, and showed him a medical
certificate from the Hospice Hospital. I have not seen the
interview yet, and am wondering if this is enough 'hard' evidence
for them, or if they need something more....[1]

THE COMPLAINT

I stood shocked before this wave of terrible cruelty for the
umteenth time. After all the disappointments I appealed again to
the Ministry of Police. I told in detail of my visits to jail, what
I saw, and demanded that a medical check-up be held immediately

---

1. Since this was written, I have seen an article in The Observer
in which Atwal's testimony was mentioned.

for all those on whom the marks were still visible on their bodies.

In the meantime I met again in Ramallah another administrative prisoner, Abdallah al-Beraat. His wife stood outside the walls of the jail. Walid and I interviewed Abdallah and heard the following story from his mouth:

During the first four days of his detention, between 5th and 9th May, he was held, naked, in the solitary confinement wing of Ramallah prison. He was beaten all over, including on the soles of his feet, loins and sexual organs.

Abdallah complained to the doctor and was given sedatives.

On the night of 7-8 May after these tortures, and after being forced by the investigators to stand continually, he collapsed. During the whole time he was blindfolded with a kafieh, even during meals. He was also beaten about the head with a stick, slapped in the face and beaten about the ears. As a result his hearing was damaged.

On 9 May he was transferred to Bethlehem jail. On the way there the policeman kicked and beat him all over while he was tied in a sack and blindfolded.

In Bethlehem prison he was sent to the dungeon, where he was held twenty days.

On 19 June he was transferred to Hebron prison. There he was abused by the investigators, specially by an officer who, according to his description, was light skinned, dark haired, sturdily built and about twenty-five years old. This officer continually threatened him, saying they should smash his bones and lamenting that he was not allowed to do so...

His investigators made him face the wall, and beat the back of his neck so that his forehead knocked against the wall.

On 25 June, the prisoner was again transferred to Ramallah. There the torture stopped, but he expressed to me his fear that the injuries remained.

Thus the system repeats itself, except that Abdallah was not in military jail, and was not harmed so much as the other prisoners for whom I complained. His hearing, however,

had been damaged and this we could tell during the interview. I
made an official complaint concerning Abdallah and demanded
that he be given a medical check-up. The replies were not late in
arriving and this time, as on innumerable occasions in the past,
the answer was that there was no basis for my clients' complaints.
As for those on whom the marks were still visible, such as
Suliman, Gamal Fretah and Halil Hajazi, there was no medical
examination.

I decided this time, for the first time in all these years,
to appeal to the High Court of Justice, which could order the
Minister of Police to set up an investigating committee to look
into the complaints. I had no other legal remedy open to me.
In my plea I relied on what H. Nakara, Ali Rafa and Fahum had
seen and heard during my absence. I demanded an investigation
and showed the Court how the police were evading the issue.

In this way an order nisi, demanding investigation of
my complaints, was given. Abroad, the appeal was mentioned
in the press, but in Israel it was written about half-heartedly at
first, then afterwards complete silence.

The investigation began, and it convinced all those who
still deluded themselves that there was a trace of honour in such
dealings.

First, I was myself investigated by a senior police
officer from Tel Aviv. It was an interesting experience. I saw
the investigator of these crimes trying to conceal them. The
investigation lasted several hours and during it I described everything I had seen. I also emphasized that I had seen it all in the
presence of a Shin Beit official called Abu Nabil. The investigators said immediately that Abu Nabil denies it. "If this is so,
your Abu Nabil must have temporarily lost his wits, because he
sat with me and heard me and saw me..." In the end the investigator told me that the complainants had inflicted the bodily
injuries that I had seen (he didn't dare say I was lying !) on themselves, with their own hands to blacken the investigators' repu-
tation and that of the Israeli Government.

The investigation of the complainants themselves was even more 'objective'. It turned out that their investigator was none other than Ben Yitzhak, known for his hatred of Arabs and Communists.

At first the complainants did not want to talk to him at all, but after becoming acquainted with him, they decided to give him evidence in their own hand-writing, in Arabic.

I demanded that the Court disqualify Ben Yitzhak, and Judge H Cohen appeared inclined to understand me and even gave expression to this. But it was decided to allow the investigation to continue and only afterwards to evaluate it.

The reply submitted to the Supreme Court by the Committee was detailed, but extremely evasive. The Shin Beit were portrayed as infants who could not harm a soul, and who were none the less forced to admit that Suliman had been handcuffed and that his hands had been tied for several days, but that it was to make sure that he did not escape. The accusations of the complainants were described as 'poisonous propaganda' and the complainants themselves as 'dangerous to the security of the state'.

In a hearing that took place in the Supreme Court, the President of the Panel, H Cohen, after I had told him that this was not an investigating committee but a joke, said that 'Any other committee would almost certainly have made the same findings'. He also added that it was difficult to prove my claims. I felt that I was up against a blank wall. The plea was rejected.

And thus the police and the Shin Beit acquitted themselves and could be happy about their achievements. But this was the superficial view, for the matter of the plea caught the attention of many people in Israel who doubted the integrity of the police. The story also reached the foreign press, who stated that only an independent investigation committee could investigate without bias.

The Israeli press responded to the termination of the hearing in almost complete silence. The word 'torture' must not be mentioned.

I had hoped that we might have had in our hands the

power to stop the torture machine, if only for a short time, to save the prisoners, both now and in the future, from some of their suffering.

BASHIR AL-BARGUTI

His name is Bashir al-Barguti. He arrived a few months ago from the East Bank, under the programme for the unity of families. Known as a Communist and as one of the leaders of the Party, his previous record is long[1]: Bashir had spent time in jails in Zarka, Amman, Jafar, Ramallah and Jerusalem. Incidentally, the records of almost all the new prisoners 'suspected of being Communists or of belonging to the National Palestinian Front' are like this. Bashir was a prisoner under King Hussein from 1957-1965. For this reason, he is very suspect to the Shin Beit...

I had never met him before. The family came to me immediately after his arrest, full of fear for his fate. And here began the usual delaying tactics to prevent me seeing him immediately.

After many formal applications it was announced that Bashir was in Ramallah prison. There, they refused to receive a letter of request for an interview, demanding that it be sent by mail. Only after the submission of the complaint at issue could the letter be received by the administrative board of Ramallah prison. By this time the refusal had come, as was intended, so that the Shin Beit could stall for time, from the legal adviser to the districts of Judea and Samaria(the West Bank). He refused in principle to speak with Yona, the secretary, or with

---

1. In criminal cases it is the custom, before sentence is read, that the plaintiff submit a record of previous convictions, if any.

Walid, the trainee, but only with me, knowing that during working hours I make my visits to the prisons and cannot get in touch with him. Once again telegrams, protests, appeals to the Communist Knesset members. This time I also appealed to Shulamit Aloni's party and requested her help. One hundred and eighty - six members of the Barguti family inside and outside the West Bank published a proclamation to the public demanding Bashir's release.

After all this my visit to Bashir was allowed for 12 August 1974 at Ramallah prison in the presence of the Shin Beit official Abu Nabil.

I arrived at the prison; the family remained near the gate. The meeting was to take place in the courtyard. A table and chairs were set out. Bashir was brought to me accompanied by Abu Nabil. Average in height, about 40, he is well-mannered. "Are you OK ?" I ask him. From the answer "Yes" I understand immediately that this time there was no torture, and something rejoiced in me. Abu Nabil asks me what I want to hear. "The truth, Abu Nabil, nothing but the truth. If it happens that you haven't beaten him, whether by accident or not, that's good !"

Bashir looks at me, and I see that he is testing me. This testing look is one of Bashir's distinguishing characteristics. It is said that eyes are the mirror of one's soul. Bashir's mirror is a special one - knowing how to hide what is inside while searching for the thoughts of others.

Bashir immediately declared that his arrest was political. He appealed in a letter to his party in Amman, and asked that it be sent by way of an engineer in the Nablus municipality, Abbas Abed al-Haq. Included in it was a request for an appeal to progressive forces in Israel, expressing solidarity with their struggle against the latest arrests and trying to find a common language with them in finding a peaceful solution to the conflict. 'I request that you appeal in my name to people like Lova Eliav, Uri Avneri, and Shulamit Aloni, to meet me to discuss the torture', added Bashir.

Abu Nabil recorded everything. I was convinced that before me was an extremely well informed man who knew what was going on in Israel, about the political forces working within it, and who was striving to meet such forces outside.

We part, and I warn Abu Nabil that the treatment of Bashir must not deteriorate. He smiles and I understand that this one at least has been saved from the hands of the investigators.

SCENES FROM GAZA

A short while ago, Mufid Abu Ramadan[1] a young educated man and an administrative prisoner was released from prison. Two

---

1. The Military Governor made a tempting offer to Mufid, a young economics graduate of an East German university: to return to East Germany 'voluntarily'. Mufid emphatically rejected it and said, "This is my homeland, why should I leave it?" After the offer came the threat - that if Mufid did not listen to their 'advice' they would keep him in administrative detention for two years.

Mufid told the Governor of Gaza that he saw his detention as an attempt to imprison progressive political thought, an act that would harm both peoples, and the prospects of peace.

The other prisoners connected with this incident were sentenced to prison for their membership of the 'National Front' in Gaza.

other prisoners were brought from Gaza prison to its military courthouse which was packed with people from Gaza. In the indictment they were accused of belonging to the National Palestinian Front, of publishing a political newspaper, of enlisting friends, etc...

Lately, this type of action has become quite regular. What was new this time was that the prosecution files on these two, who firmly denied any guilt, were devoid of evidence against them. It must be noted that bringing to trial those who don't confess in the police station is a new practice of the Occupation forces, to repress progressive thought completely. The prosecution knew there was no proof at all, so the authorities tried to make Fidel Borno, one of the two, sign a voluntary expulsion order to avoid bringing him to trial. But Fidel refused, and succeeded in contacting the Red Cross and threatened to appeal to the Supreme Court. The authorities announced that the expulsion would not take place. On 29 November 1974 the two were brought to hear the indictment against them. I demanded that they be released on bail. I showed the court that Fidel Borno was ill with heart and kidney disease and that each additional day in prison endangered his life. Moreover, it was scandalous to hold people in jail on no evidence at all. The prosecutor jumps from his seat yelling "We do have evidence, we will bring the Shin Beit people here." "And where is the evidence ? Obviously I will need to study it !" I answer. The prosecutor, "You won't see it." Here the judge intervened to say that it was the right of the defence to see the complete file, but that it could be seen in this case that the file was empty. "You put foreward claims made by Yediot Aharonot, but this is a court and not a press conference. Can you prove it ?" I asked. The judge stops us and makes his decision. He openly admits that if he were a civil judge he would unhesitatingly grant the defence request and free the two. He nevertheless decides to detain them until the end of the trial, but limits their sentences to the end of November. He also ordered the prison to give medical treatment to Fidel Borno. It should be noted that the two had been detained since 12 June 1974.

After the end of the short session, the military police
agreed to allow Fidel Borno to see his young children, but not
with his wife present. After many applications his wife met him.
She fell into his arms, and could barely be separated from him.
His young daughter could not say a word because she was afraid
of the stern-faced military police, with their weapons. Even Fidel's
assurances, that they were all good people, did not help.

The parents of Said, the second man brought to trial,
were not permitted to see him. "You are not children," remarked
one of the police. The elderly mother burst into tears, the father
calmed her. In the end the heart of one of the policemen softened
and he allowed the parents to go one by one to the cell to shake
hands with their son through the bars.

THE VOLCANO

Warna, Bulgaria, November 1974. I participate as an honoured
guest of the Congress of the Federation of Democratic Youth.
Warna is a lovely vacation resort on the shores of the clear blue
Black Sea. In the halls of the Congress a well-known French
lawyer tells us how he defends political prisoners in Chile.
Yoram Gojansky and Salam Gobran, members of the Israeli
delegation, appear in the Committee against Occupation and call
for the recognition of Palestinian rights and for a just peace for
all the peoples in the area. I was chosen to appear in a special full
session devoted to solidarity with the struggle of the Arab peoples
and the Palestinian people for their rights and a just peace. I
speak from my experience, and bring greetings to the Congress

from those behind bars. I call for a solution that recognizes the
rights of the Palestinians as well as the rights of Israel. One after
another, greetings from Prime Ministers and representatives of
youth from every continent are read, expressing solidarity and
censuring the Israeli Government's policy. In the same spirit
the Palestinian representative speaks to the Congress. In the
hallway is an exhibit showing women and children killed by Israeli
bombings of refugee camps in Lebanon.

At precisely this same time the UN discussion of the
Palestinian problem was about to begin. News items arrive from
Israel. The hall is small and we follow the developments in Israel
with bated breath. News agencies report that the excitement
began in Nablus on the eve of the UN discussion. Thousands of
proclamations calling for residents to strike in support of the
Palestinian delegation to the UN were distributed.

On the opening day of the UN debate, thousands of Nablus
high-school students went on a stormy demonstration in the streets;
they waved Palestinian flags and carried pictures of PLO leaders.
The police attacked and arrested hundreds of pupils among the
demonstrators.

During the entire morning all the shops and factories in the
town were closed, despite warnings from the Government that harsh
measures would be taken against the demonstrators, and that they
would have their businesses confiscated. There were strikes in
most of the schools.

The Military Governor demanded from the mayor of
al-Masari that he intervene to calm things down, but the mayor
explained that the municipality could not influence the inflamed
people, and that this was not his job.

That same day the military court of Nablus sentenced
24 students to seven days in prison or fines of up to 1,000 Israeli
pounds each. Ten of the arrested who did not pay the fine remained
in jail.

The next day also stormy demonstrations continued in
the city, and again police forces attacked them, injuring two

people and arresting twenty. The arrested were brought to trial
in military courts and sentenced to twenty days in prison or fines
of 1, 000 Israeli pounds each.

The next day heavy terms of six months in prison were
imposed.

The arrests and injuries of the students made the mood
even more stormy. The demonstrations increased the next day,
and the students were on almost total strike from their studies.
This was in spite of Government warnings of closing the schools
till the end of the school year. Leaving aside all the anger against
the Occupation Government and its cruelty, the residents expressed their desire for peace and their certainty that the recognition
of the Arab Palestinian people would bring peace closer. Young
people in Nablus bore witness to this when they told a Maariv
correspondent: "When Arafat spoke at the UN the whole Arab
world held its breath. He proved to the whole world that he wants
peace. The Israeli Government will be forced to speak with the
PLO: without a solution to the Palestinian problem, peace in the
area will never come."

Over the weekend the demonstrations spread to the rest
of the West Bank, as well as the main streets of Jenin, Hebron,
Ramallah, al-Bira and Halhul. In Jenin the border police - while
trying to break up the demonstrations - caused the death of
Mintaha Awad al-Hourani, a fifteen-year-old student. She and
three other girls were run over by one of the three vehicles of
the border police that burst into the crowd of demonstrators.

After these bloody events, the mood was even more
feverish, and the number of demonstrators grew. Police forces,
unable to control or disband the masses, shot into the air. But
no-one was put off by this, and the funeral of the young girl, in
which thousands of residents took part, turned into an angry demonstration against the Occupation Government. After the girl's
death, proclamations calling for a general strike were distributed in the cities of the West Bank.

The Mayor of Jenin and the Secretary of its Bureau of

Industry sent a memorandum to the West Bank Commander in which they protested that "a military vehicle deliberately entered the demonstrators and as a result the pupil was killed."

In Hebron, stormy demonstrations and strikes in the schools took place through the pupils' rage at the death of their comrade in Jenin and the injuries of others. Many businesses and shops closed down in solidarity with the demonstrators, in spite of Government threats. A number of demonstrators set fire to the Hebron "Settlers" restaurant near the Tomb of the Patriarchs.

In an attempt to repress the demonstration, the police forces injured eleven students, who were brought to the city hospital. Dozens of students were arrested and sentenced to terms of one to three months or fines up to 1,700 Israeli pounds. A curfew was enforced in the city centre.

In Ramallah demonstrations had already begun on 13 November and they grew as a result of the riots from the Occupation forces against the residents. Students from the Teacher's Seminar and from the UNRWA school added their numbers. They carried Palestinian flags and the police tried to disperse them, using clubs and guns.

As a result ten students were injured; pupils and adults were arrested and given sentences of up to six months and fines of 500 Israeli pounds each.

In Halhul and Dora schools were on strike and high-school pupils demonstrated on the streets. Here, too, police intervened with force to disperse them. The majority of the shops in these towns went on strike. In Halhul the curfew was enforced and thirty of the demonstrators were arrested.

Additional demonstrations took place in the villages of Arabeh, Silit ed-Dahar and Kabatiya, as well as at Beir Zeit college.

Women's organizations in the West Bank and the Gaza Strip printed a proclamation in which they expressed their appreciation of the Palestinian victories at the UN, and called for the establishment of National Assemblies in the cities of the

Occupied Territories, from which an executive committee would be chosen to be responsible for activities in the territories.

At the beginning of the week most of the demonstrations and strikes took place in East Jerusalem, Bethlehem and Beit Jalla. In East Jerusalem mass demonstrations of students occurred and businesses went on strike. Police and military forces responded with violence, used water hoses, and arrested many demonstrators. They threatened the striking businessmen with confiscation of their businesses and even recorded many of their names, to take revenge on the shop-owners for the strike. Fourteen students were taken for medical treatment and three policemen were injured. About 250 students were arrested and were sentenced at 'instant' trials held until two o'clock in the morning. Fifty-four of them received six-month sentences and the rest received heavy fines or imprisonment.

In far away Bulgaria the hearts of Palestinians filled with pride for their brothers and sisters demonstrating against the Occupation. Among them are those who have been expelled from their homeland, such as Arabi Awad of Nablus, who cannot return so long as the Occupation continues.

I am with my entire family. My son Michael introduces himself to the Palestinians of his own age and to the adults. I see his eyes gaping as he hears about the injustices. Our hearts beat at the same rate, and he holds my hand. These are moments of closeness.

We separate. I hurry to return to those behind bars.

BAKR ABED AL-HAQ

Bakr Abed al-Haq is an old man from Nablus. Over 80, for

forty-eight years he had been a teacher. His two sons, Abbas and
Haldun, are in jail as administrative prisoners. The third son was
expelled by the security authorities at the beginning of November:
I had met Azam, a graduate of the Soviet University. Of course
there was no legal reason for his expulsion. The writer M Avi
Shaul spoke with the elderly father when he visited Nablus as head
of the delegation of the League of Human Rights, and this is what
the father said:

"The expulsions which took place between 1949 and 1967
and afterwards were events which happened before our very eyes,
not episodes read about in history books. How is it possible not
to understand this ?"

In connection with his sons Abbas and Haldun, still in
prison, and Azam, expelled the previous week, Bakr Abed al-Haq
says, "My son, Haldun, has been rotting in prison for eight months.
Why don't they say what he did wrong ? True, he struggled for
the right of his people to live - is nothing forbidden ? Is nothing unethical ? For eight and a half years Haldun was imprisoned
in Jordan. The torture and suffering in jail did not erase his faith.
You must be aware that Haldun and his friends are authentically
expressing our wishes, the wishes of the Arab Palestinian people.
We want one thing: to live and to live in peace. As for my son Abbas,
he is an engineer. His work is central to him. I don't know, and
I don't understand, what the point of imprisoning him was."

The wives of Abbas and Haldun took part in the conversation.
Their husbands were taken to prison while they were pregnant.
They bore their children while their fathers were still in prison.
Haldun has three children, aged 8, 4, and 4 months.

Abbas has four children, the oldest daughter 11, the
youngest 4 months.

The wives are bitter about the cruel laws that imprison
people such as their husbands without due process of law. Instead
of freeing them at the end of the period of administrative detention,
it is increased another six months. They stress their lack of
faith in the Military Government, fearing that the period of detention, ending in January 1975, will again be extended. They say,

appealing to public opinion in Israel, " Raise your voices in protest in Israel !   Don't remain silent!   Don't agree to the injustice inflicted on us !''

The women complained about what went on in the prisons. Memories of the torturing of their dear ones are still fresh in their minds. They reported that they had been allowed to visit their husbands only once a month. The procedure is that on the first Friday of the month families of convicted prisoners can visit, and on the second Friday those of the administrative prisoners. The women are bitter at the limit on clothing brought to the prison. The authorities return all or most of the clothing, and do not pass it on to the prisoners. They forbid blankets and sweaters, so necessary to the prisoners now that the days and nights are becoming cold, and winter is approaching. Abbas's wife says, "Why do the Israeli prison warders think that Arabs don't need clean clothes more often ? Why to the shirts and underwear brought to the prisoners have to be limited ? Only one vest and one shirt can be passed over each month - that isn't enough! "

Dr Samira Abu Lail, a dentist and the wife of Dr Abu Lail the paediatrician, told of her sufferings at her visit to jail..

"I well remember how I saw him after one of the strikes, growing a beard, and limping. His appearance alarmed me. He said that when the warders fed him by a tube and he objected, they grabbed his legs by force and injured them."

THE WOODEN LEG

He lies on the wooden bench in the Military Court in Lod. His name is Abd al-Rahman al-Bitar, a resident of Arab Jerusalem. He is eighty years old. His eyes are closed, his breathing heavy.

One of the policemen gives him water. Another remarks, "How
is someone like this brought here, all skin and bone ?" On the
bench near him rests a wooden leg. It is one of the man's legs,
as he has lost his own.

"He will die here," someone says.

Suddenl y the man's eyes open. A groan comes from him,
"My stomach, my stomach hurts...."

The indifferent keep quiet, the more sensitive appear
uneasy. Someone asks, "Does this old man have a lawyer ?" One
of the policemen answers, "Yes, but he hasn't come today."

The room becomes restless. Soldiers gather round the
'cage' which fences in the accused benches and the man who lies on
one of them. Suddenly the military prosecutor arrives. It appears
that he has been called urgently for consultation. He calms me,
"Volunteer to represent him today, request that he be released on
bail. I won't object and the Court will free him."

The judges enter the hall. Two policemen try to sit up
the accused, but without success. I stand up and say that in the
light of the terrible spectacle before us I volunteer to defend the
accused, though I am unclear why he was brought to trial at all.
I request that he be released on bail, and the Prosecutor agrees.

"First we will read him the indictment," says the
President of the Panel, without looking at the man. The indictment
states that before us is a 'Fatah' man who has admitted to con-
cealing arms....He is freed on bail of 2, 000 Israeli pounds.

"Please write in the finding of the court that he must be
taken to his house, that he cannot get there by himself, and that
he has no family," I request. The President writes. I ask again
that the court should see that the man is well escorted, to be
sure of his safety.

The judges leave the hall quickly, before the accused is
led out by the police, as if they preferred not to see.

The police go to him and help him fit on his wooden leg.
He stands on his one good leg supported in their arms, and they
leave the hall to the clicking sound of his wooden leg.

" It's not like that these days, when legs are properly
fitted," someone remarks appropriately.

MUHAMMAD YASIN: JANUARY 1975

The battle against the progressive forces in the occupied territories continues. In addition to the scores being held under administrative arrest, without charge or trial, there are those from
whom the Shin Beit have succeeded in wringing confessions of
guilt to be used in evidence against them in military court.

One of these trials concluded on 23 January 1975 in the
military court at Nablus, against Muhammad Yasin, an engineer
from Nablus accused of belonging to the "military faction of the
Jordanian Communist Party, known as the National Palestinian Front,
attempting to enlist two other people, and of being trained in the
use of arms in the USSR."

How is it to be proved in court, in contradiction to the
facts, that the National Palestinian Front is a 'military faction'
of the Communist Party ? Nothing is simpler: first of all a
'confession' is wrung from Yasin, through beatings and torture
and complete isolation from his family and from me for about
two months. In this 'confession' the military faction is mentioned. Furthermore, when Yasin comes to court and shows the
marks of cigarettes extinguished on his body by his investigators,
describes the Shin Beit personnel who abused him, giving exact
dates of the events, the court – this time through the new Presid-
dent of the military courts in Judea and Samaria, Colonel Gershon
Orion – determines that a 'preliminary trial' concerning the
police receiving Yasin's confession will not be held, that his
claim that he was forced to confess will not be accepted, and

that they will automatically accept the confession as valid evidence, contrary to custom.   The judge suggests that the institution of this 'trial' be cancelled at once as being a wearisome and unnecessary proceeding, even though it is the cornerstone of the Anglo-Saxon legal system, used alike in Israel's military and civil courts. In this way the judge seeks to replace the legislator.

The second source brought to 'substantiate' the evidence of the existence of the military faction is a Shin Beit 'expert' on 'illegal organizations', called to tell us about the 'military faction' without specifying a single name, or mentioning a single fact.   When in the cross-examination I pressed him to reveal the source of his information, the judge came quickly to his aid and forbade the question.   The witnesses' evidence is heard behind closed doors in the interests of 'personal safety'.

Yasin was found guilty on all counts, and the judge did not even refer to the accused's claims, under oath, that he was beaten and tortured.

The military prosecutor, Major Farkash, encouraged by the sharp words of the sentence and the advice of the president (an unacceptable practice, which I brought up on the spot) requested the maximum sentence - ten years   imprisonment. When he sensed that the reaction was one of shock, he 'justified' his request by saying that "our first duty is to the public.   Men such as Yasin are like a time-bomb: they harm the public among whom they live much more than they harm the Government.   I will explain myself: road checks on local residents, asking for identification, etc... That same resident of Nablus, travelling to Tel Aviv to buy goods, would prefer not to be stopped by that same soldier to be searched, and not to be looked at with suspicion.   The people from the territories don't expect people like Yasin to be found in their midst.   A person like this goes abroad to train in arms, to be 'loaded' with ideas, and thus even if he is not active, he is a great danger, and needs to be kept far away from the public."

It must be noted that in the past similar statements have been made in connection with similar offences.

In my summary, I said that the merchants of Nablus, who are said not to want him in their midst since he interferes with their profits, have expressed their opinion on this more than once. The Occupation, and not Yasin, is the source of their troubles. It is the Occupation that is like a time-bomb, and not Yasin.

In conclusion I referred to precedents from military courts in the area, in which sentences of a few months, or at most a year, were given for similar or identical offences. "If you accept the cruel request of the prosecutor, and give heavy punishment for non-violent acts, it will only encourage those who claim that there is no political way to struggle for the recognition of their rights."

Yasin rises from his seat and says that he has not endangered anyone's safety, that he is faithful to his people and to his land, and that he believes in the brotherhood of all nations.

The president stops him, "You talk about what you stand for. But what about your crimes ?"

Yasin: "I have committed no crime against anyone."

After consultation the sentence was passed. "In this case we must attach much more importance to the deterrence than to the punishment of the accused. We are talking of the foundation of a new illegal organization, the National Palestinian Front- a phenomenon we are encountering for the first time. The accused expressed no regret when given the chance to speak for the first time, and thus it appears to us that it is desirable to take him far away from the public for a long period, to stop his subversive activities." Yasin received a sentence of eight years. This was an unprecedented punishment for such an offence. In addition, there is no Supreme Court of Appeal in the occupied territories to which one can appeal against such an injustice.

It is plain that this drastic sentence was just one link in a chain of injustice disguised as a trial. The one-sided press reporting, which gave no account of the defence version of events or of the words of the accused, points to the intention of the authorities to manipulate public opinion.

The court decision left the Nablus public dazed. I made a
firm commitment to myself to do everything to get the sentence
annulled. Although over the years I had never so far succeeded in
obtaining an annullment for any decision, I still decided to go to
the High Court of Justice.

I submitted a request for annullment the next day, in which
I relied on the legal mistakes of the president in not conducting the
'preliminary' trial, in silencing the accused, and in his unprecedented
verdict dictated by completely illegal considerations.

I also made a report to the French journalist Eric Rouleau
of Le Monde[1] about the results of the trial, which he had requested
from me when he was present at one of the sessions.

A second event awaited Yasin, to which I will return later.

HALIL RASHMAWI

It is not enough when the occupation government imprisons scores
of innocent progressives in administrative detention without trial,
enraging residents of the territories and resulting in protests by
democratic sections of the Israeli public.

Now, too, every meeting between attorney and prisoner
is deliberately delayed, thus taking place a considerable time
after arrest.

Only on 18 October 1974 did I receive permission to see
two of my clients, residents of Bethlehem, who had been arrested
on 28 September. The meeting took place in Ramallah prison, in

---

1. He wrote a long article on the trial, and one which was not at
all flattering to the court.

the presence of the Shin Beit official Abu Nabil, and his presence
was the condition for the visit.

Halil Anton Rashmawi told me that he saw sunlight that
day for the first time since his arrest. For two weeks he had
been in solitary confinement; now he was being held in a dark cell,
though not alone, and even a daily outing was not permitted.

"Yesterday, for the first time, I had a bath," says Halil.
He has a stomach complaint, but has received no medical treatment at all. "They asked me why I went to study in the Soviet
Union, and about my political views and connections." Halil has
an MA in agronomy from the USSR. He teaches in several schools
and at Bethlehem University.

His father told me, "They came to our house at night.
Why do they have to do it at night ? They surrounded the house
as if someone was trying to escape. They asked me about Halil
and I told them he was asleep, not trying to escape, and asked
them what he had done. They didn't answer me, but went straight
to Halil's library. He has a lot of books. They glanced through
them till they found two that interested them. They were by Lenin.
I asked why they were taking them. They answered that they were
books that endangered the security of the state. I asked why, in
that case, they were sold in bookshops, and what Lenin could do
to harm Israel. They didn't answer. They took my son Halil,
who studied for many years to work for his people. You should
see how anxious his students at the University and the other schools
where he teaches are for his return."

RENEWAL OF THE ADMINISTRATIVE ARRESTS

Time passes and the news items get worse. The authorities lengthened the sentences of the administrative prisoners by an additional six months without process of law, at the end of the three-month period.

Among the detained were Ibrahim al-Jolani, Taher Arafeh, Majid Abu Sariya, Mahmud Shkair, Asad Snokrot, Amer Sharabati, Halil Tuma, Basman Abu Armeleh, Majid Sidar, Abd al-Karim al-Shaludi, Omar Odeh, Karim Hamdan, Muhammad Taher Shaludi, Yahia Abu Sharif, Husni Hadad, an engineer, Muhammad Sada, Atallah al-Rasmawi, Abd al-Majid Hamdan, Abdallah Abd al-Majid, Adnan Majid, Secretary of the Construction Workers' Union, Ghassan al-Harb, Adal Mahmud, Hussein Farah al-Tawil, Dr Farha Abu Lail, Haldun Abd al-Haq, Laviv Fakr al-Din, Jamal Fretah, Abd al-Basat al-Hiyat, Halil Hajazi, Yakoub Farah, Farouk al-Salfiti, Adel Barguti, Faizir Rajab al-Aruri, a teacher at Beir Zeit College, Abdallah al-Siriani, Suliman al-Rashid Najab, Hader al-Alam, Bahaj al-Shuibi, Maisra al-Shuibi, Mahmud Karame, Suliman al-Beraat, Ahmad Samra, and others.

The League for Human and Civil Rights called for a demonstration in front of the Knesset. Despite stormy weather and flooding the League of Jews and Arabs, among them students and many young people, protested at the injustice, and expressed solidarity with the families of the prisoners.

The large group of relatives, wives, mothers and sisters with scarves round their heads, stood out, and their presence moved the protesters.

In short speeches from those active in the League, it was pointed out that the administrative prisoners' only crime was their objection to occupation.

Knesset member Tawfiq Zayad went out to the demonstration and expressed his support and solidarity with the protesters. Determined not to rest until the arbitrarily jailed Palestinians had been freed, the demonstrators at last dispersed.

PROTEST

A notice was published in Ha-Aretz by a group of people on 30
January 1975 appealing to the Israeli authorities.

The signatories were the professors A A Simon, L N
Posner, A Sachs, H Oppenheimer, S Vogel, Y Danciger, Y Sadan,
D Amit, K Altman, Dr B Cohen, Dr S Balas, Dr Y Lef, N Yalin
Mor, B Evron, P Yalin Mor, A Zichroni, Y Amitai, A Goldreich,
A Paska, A Burstein, A Kenan, B Cohen, M Barzili, Y Chen and
Yevi.

In a telegram   sent to the Prime Minister, Yitzhak
Rabin, by the Secretary of the World Council for Peace, it was
stated that 'The World Council for Peace sharply criticizes the
renewal of arbitrary arrests of Palestinian patriots from the West
Bank.' It demanded that human rights be honoured, that the per-
secution end, and that all Palestinian prisoners be freed at once.

In the meantime the administrative prisoners called a
week-long hunger strike protesting at the extending of their sentences and demanding to be freed. This was the second hunger
strike of their detention, and it had repercussions for the Israeli
public. It was impossible to hide the strike and even the establishment press was forced to report it.

The following notice appeared in Ha-Aretz on 6 February
1975:

HUNGER STRIKE

Dozens of administrative prisoners detained in jails in Israel
and the occupied territories for nine months without trial,
have initiated a week-long hunger strike in protest and have
demanded to be freed.

FREE THEM OR BRING THEM TO TRIAL

Signed:
Professor Hanan Oppenheimer   Dr Drin-Dravkin

Uri Avneri

Professor L N Posner

Nathan Yalin Mor

Professor Dan Meron

Meir Pail, Knesset member

Professor Arie Sachs

Amos Kenan

Professor Yitzhak Danciger

Danny Karavan

Professor Shaul Vogel

Gershon Plotkin

Dr Benjamin Cohen

Shmuel Mikonis

Professor Daniel Amit

Avraham Paska

Dr Yehuda Meltzer

Latif Dori

Simcha Flapan

Avraham Levenbraun, Knesset
member

Dr Israel Lef

Ester Vilneska

Dr Shmuel Amir

Yitzhak Hizkieh

Niba Lanir

Dan Kadar

Professor Kalman Altman

Arthur Goldreich

Kohi (K Harel)

Danny Petter

Ruth Luvitch

Benjamin Gonen

Victor Seigalman

Feiler Eliezer

Uzi Burstein

Dr Varda Cohen

Eli Kenan

Yaakov Hen

Beni Tomkin

David Heitner

Yosef Hochman (K Harel)

Zvi Brightstein

Avraham Lansman

Yoram Gozinsky

Moshe Gabsa

Haas Avraham

Elikim Margaliot

Tamar Peleg-Shrik

Yevi

When I visited the different jails, the prisoners asked me to relay their gratitude to those who had raised their voices in support of their freedom.

YAWNING IN COURT

The trials of the two youths from the refugee camp of Arub,
Abdallah Mahmud Abdallah Abd al-Aziz and Hasan Muhammad Zakut
al-Badawi, took place in the military court in Hebron on 12 September. Abdallah was charged with belonging to an illegal organization, whose name and nature he knew nothing of, and with
training in arms outside the area. The second youth was charged
with training in arms. The additional charge against Abdallah
was "making contact with a hostile organization outside the area, "
in that he met his cousin in Amman when there was good reason to
believe that the cousin belonged to a hostile organization. It was
pointed out that Abdallah's cousin had been expelled to Jordan by
the occupation authorities several years ago. His name is
Muhammad Hasan Diab. The accused claimed, by way of me,
that accusations of this kind of 'contact' could be levelled against
every resident of the West Bank who meets relatives 'when there
is good reason to believe' that they belong to organizations that
do not sympathize with the occupation.

During the discussion, the president of the panel suddenly
got angry, and demanded that the proceedings stop, saying, "What
is happening ? They can't stop yawning in court. It doesn't fit
the occasion. At least they could do it quietly ! Please translate
to the audience that their yawning in intolerable !" The translator
does so, adding his own personal touch, saying that it is forbidden
to utter a word in the hall of the court and that anyone disobeying
this order will be removed immediately.

The accused were found guilty and sentenced - Abdallah
to a year in prison and Hasan to seven months. The two also
received suspended sentences so that they would not come into
contact again....

Thus the occupiers determined that the only ones 'fit for
contact' were those who co-operated with them. And they are
certainly difficult to find in the occupied territories, and only
a few can be found outside. The rest are treated as lepers.

MAJDAL SHAMS ONCE MORE

On 19 December 1974 in the military court in Majdal Shams the trials of the two youths were concluded. The two, from the village, were Nazia Abu Ziad and Salman Fakri Din, the first aged fifteen and a half, the second 20 years old. Nazia is accused of passing on information to the Syrian Intelligence and of infiltrating three times from Syria; Salman is accused of passing on information, of armed infiltration and of being in possession of grenades.

From the beginning the authorities' interest in Salman was clear, as his articles had appeared in <u>Al-Itihad.</u> In addition, his proud silence in court aroused the anger of the authorities.

This anger must be understood in relation to the situation in the village at the time: after many years of occupation the authorities had succeeded in appointing a 'puppet' local council, despite the opposition of local residents, in order to demonstrate their 'firm control' in the area. Lately, members of the council (former prisoners, those accused of spying for Israel...) had been receiving written threats that they would be harmed if they continued their work. In the neighbouring village of Bokata similar threats were received by members of the council. All this, of course, caused the authorities uneasiness, when it was proved that the council did not represent the residents, but themselves alone.

At the trial, the accused refused to give evidence under oath. "The accused's words are not believed anyway. That being so, why should we swear to them ?" Nazia Abu Ziad denied the accusations against him and described what he had undergone in the investigation, when he had been held in Akko; how he had been cruelly beaten by the Shin Beit, how they had spat in his food so that he could not eat it. Salman was stopped when he began to speak of the behaviour of the Shin Beit, as it was claimed that this was not a 'little or preliminary trial'.

The accused were charged on all counts. The prosecutor

demanded an extremely heavy penalty, so that Israel's security
would not be endangered, since 'it is known that our security
situation is not good." In my submission, I relied on precedents,
and on the Geneva Convention, which does not require loyalty to
the occupying nation. I ridiculed the quality of the 'evidence' on
which the accused were convicted, mainly the passing on to the
Syrians their 'discovery' of Israeli Defence Force bases in the
villages of Bokata and Masada. "These bases were Syrian bases
captured by the Israeli army after the occupation, so their presence is scarcely a sensation as far as the Syrians are concerned."

The judges, headed by Major Akiva Ben Haim, pointed
out that the offences were serious, but they would take into account
Nazia's youth and sentence him to three years in prison plus five
years suspended. Salman was sentenced to five years in prison
with seven years suspended.

Someone in the audience remarked that the sentences
indicated very long-range planning. Another remarked that the
two neither pleaded for mercy nor expressed regret. Everyone spoke
of Salman, who, during the break, said that he felt he had fulfilled
his duty and that he hoped a just peace would prevail in the area.

THE FARHAT FAMILY

Amin Taha Farhat, an 18-year-old youth from East Jerusalem,
was arrested a month ago, and since then has been held in the
Jerusalem Detention House in the Russian Compound.

In the meantime the Muslim festival of Eid al-Adha
arrived, and it had been promised to Amin's family that they
could visit their son, as was their custom.

Early on the morning of the first day of the festival,

members of the family arrived with sweets and a bundle of clothing.
The 70-year-old father and the mother waited in the cold and knocked
on the door... but in vain.

On 29 December 1974 I was promised, as Amin's representative, that the long-awaited visit would take place on 30 December
'at 8 o'clock exactly', with the approval of Inspector Tal of the
Investigations Department. But at 8 o'clock exactly Mr Tal went
out to a meeting; only after much protest did the visit take place
at 12 noon on that day. The father, the only one to receive permission to visit, entered the detention house, and then it became
known that Amin had been transferred the previous day, the 29th,
to the prison at Kfar Yona...

It was impossible to visit him in Kfar Yona prison, as he
was brought to it only in transit on his way to Damun.

Small things, at first glance, but how much suffering they
can cause. Dozens of people crowded into my office. Countless
phone calls, and the person responsible is at some mysterious
meeting every time they hear the call is from my office.

Yona, the dedicated secretary, became a wailing wall
to each of these despairing families, who walk for days in the
hope of paying a visit (which is, incidentally, guaranteed to them
by law).

THE 16-YEAR-OLD GIRL

There was an unusual sight in the military court at Lod on 15
January 1975: in the dock sat a young boy and girl, Ihmal Taha,
aged 16, and Usma Hasima, aged 17. They exchanged glances
and every once in a while, a few sentences. Ihmal, who appears
much younger than her age, and Usma, dressed in prison garb,

look as if they have come by mistake. Even the policemen remark,
" Why do they have to bring children like them here?"   On 31 October 1974 they had been sentenced to imprisonment for their membership of the National Front in East Jerusalem. Their membership
of the organization lasted about a month and a half and was not
accompanied by any act whatsoever.

Ihmal had a blind mother and a paralysed sister, and the young
girl is an indispensible help to them. All this was brought to the
knowledge of the court. In addition, this time the probation officer's
report was in Ihmal's favour. It was unusual among surveys of
this sort of so-called 'security offence' in that it did not recommend
that Ihmal receive a prison sentence. But despite all this Ihmal
was sentenced to nine months and Usma to a year and a half. The
two submitted an appeal against the sentence.

At the appeal I pointed out the defects in the sentence of
the military court at Lod, as it had not taken into account the
probation officer's report nor the circumstances of the offence
and its extenuation conditions.

The judges withdrew to take counsel. After two hours
Usma Hasima's appeal was rejected. Concerning Ihmal's, the
judges were divided (unusual in the Court of Appeals) and two
sentences were given - one by the majority and one by the minority: the majority reduced her sentence to four months, while
the minority decided that she must serve her full term of nine
months and that the military court at Lod had been justified in its
decisions.

And so Ihmal's appeal was accepted. Usma's appeal
was rejected unanimously. Those who expected her to be over-
joyed proved wrong. Though her parents' faces lit up when they
heard the news, Ihmal asked sadly, " Why was my sentence reduced by five whole months and Usma's not even by one?"

BASHIR AL-BARGUTI

Bashir has been imprisoned for more than six months. We had
conversed a good deal, and it was clear that his investigators
had failed to make him appear guilty of establishing an 'armed
organization', of making 'plans of attack' or of other acts attributed to him. It appeared that their failure might bring about his
release, but this did not happen: the military prosecution decided
to bring him to trial and on 12 September 1974 an indictment was
submitted against him at the military court of Ramallah, in which
he was accused of spying and of writing and sending a letter containing details of the activities of the Security Forces against
subversive movements in the area. In the letter Bashir had
written of the arrest of people such as Suliman Najab, and that
it was his opinion that such people in the occupied territories
ought to appeal to Israeli progressive public opinion, to the Israeli
working class, and to all those who want peace, to explain to them the
problem of the rights of the Palestinian Arab people, and to ask
them for support in matters affecting their cause. It was clear
that the accusation was a cheap fabrication. Many lawyers expressed their willingness to defend Barguti. The official press
widely reported that a unique sort of trial for spying was about to
take place in Ramallah. And on 27 September 1974 the newspaper
Davar wrote that this would be 'The first indictment against a
Communist public figure in the West Bank.'
    Rakah, the Israeli Communist Party, demanded that the
trial be cancelled. In a front-page article appearing under the
headline "A Staged Trial" in the party newspaper Zu Ha-Derech
on 2 October 1974 it was stated:

The administrative arrests and tortures aroused a wave of
protests in Israel and in many countries of the world.
    When Rakah brought up the subject on the daily agenda of
the Knesset, Shimon Peres, Minister of Defence, tried to
deny the facts of torture with hardened impudence, despite

the decisive proof that was brought. At this he promised that
the administrative prisoners who were not guilty would be freed
and those who were found guilty would be brought to trial.

But neither of these things happened. The administrative
prisoners were not freed and not a single one was brought to
trial. It was proved beyond all doubt that these arrests were
acts of premeditated political oppression to break the progressive
forces and supporters of peace among the Palestinian people.
It was also clearly proved that the suggestions by the Minister
of Defence and by the media that the administrative prisoners
were connected with acts carried out against Israeli citizens
were lies.

After the arbitrary political nature of the arrests was proved
beyond a doubt, the Minister of Defence tried to stage a trial...
concerning the spying charge against Bashir al-Barguti.

But this staged trial, if they dare to go ahead with it, would
surely act as a boomerang against oppression and the occupation
government. Every upright Israeli must condemn this ridiculous
and wicked attempt to connect Bashir al-Barguti, a progressive
public figure and supporter of peace, a journalist and economist,
with this false accusation.

We demand that the staged trial of Bashir al-Barguti be
stopped immediately, that he be freed from arbitrary imprisonment, and that all political prisoners be freed.

Shimon Peres, Minister of Defence, a known hawk, has acted
to increase the oppression in the occupied territories. But
public opinion in Israel and throughout the world censures acts
of oppression to a greater and greater degree. No increase in
oppression can eliminate the national existence of the Palestinian people or destroy the progressive forces and supporters of
peace within it.

The government, in increasing the oppression in the occupied
territories, as part of its wrong-headed policy, works against
the real interests of Israel and of peace.

We call on all supporters of peace in Israel to raise their

voices in protest and to demand an end to the staged trial against Bashir al-Barguti, to demand that all administrative prisoners be freed, and to stop the policy of oppression and the sabotaging of peace.

But the trial was not stopped, and began on 19 January 1975 in the military court in Ramallah. Eleven lawyers, Jewish and Arab, volunteered to defend him, and in preliminary consultation I was appointed co-ordinator for the defence. The lawyers were Hanna Nikara, Abd al-Hafiz Darawsha (who were present in the first session) as well as Avraham Melamed, Gazi Kfir, Walid al-Fahum, Muhammad al-Haj, Muhammad Miari, Azat Darawsha, Hasan Nassar, Anis Shakur and Atmana Mansarat.

The hall was packed with Bashir's relatives. The chief editor of the newspaper Al-Itihad, the Communist Party leader Amil Habibi, was also among the crowd.

The session opened. There are three judges. The President is Colonel Gershon Orion. Bashir is ordered to rise. The military prosecutor accuses him of 'spying', using as evidence a letter written to one of his friends in Amman, which was seized by the authorities. What was written in this letter ? The letter included things published in the press and heard in the Knesset itself concerning the wave of arrests and tortures of members of the "National Palestinian Front". In his letter Bashir al-Barguti had written about the occupation authorities' attempt to accuse Communists of military activities. Here Barguti expressed his opinion about the need to appeal to workers and to all people of good will in Israel, in solidarity with the prisoners, in support of future peace and also to international public opinion, to save the prisoners from torture.

The military prosecutor brought one of the Shin Beit to give evidence in a closed session. But the military court allowed the evidence to become public, as it did not appear to include any 'security' matter. The only thing the evidence stated was that Bashir al-Barguti was one of the leaders of the Jordanian

Communist party and that his friend in Amman was also a leader.
The Defence asked what kind of 'spying' it was when two leaders
of a party wished to exchange opinions ?

At the end of the hearing of the defence evidence, Nikara
asked that the charges be dismissed, as no grounds for prosecution
had been proved.

But the military prosecutor recalled the words of an
Israeli lawyer in a previous case – that, according to the law of
'National Security', the kind of information sent abroad is unim-
portant; even if it concerns the agricultural products used in
farming, it is in the hands of the Israeli Intelligence alone to
decide if that information endangers state security or not.

The prosecutor admitted that the occupation government
wanted to hide the wave of arrests and torture from the world.
Therefore, the information that Barguti had passed on was a danger to the 'security of the area'.

The court rejected the defence claim that nothing had been
proved against Barguti, and decided to resume the trial on 2 February, when his affirmation would be heard. Silence reigned.
Bashir said that although he had written a letter to the Jordanian
Communist Party about the arrests in the occupied territories,
the names he had given had all appeared in the Israeli and international press. He said that he knew these prisoners personally,
as well as being familiar with their views in favour of a just
peace, the right of Israel to self-determination, and the establishment of a Palestinian state alongside Israel.

Walid translated this, and both judges and journalists
showed interest. Bashir's voice was calm and confident. He
continued, louder, "Seventeen years ago, in this same courtroom,
on this very spot, I was sentenced by the Jordanian court to sixteen years in prison for the crime of Communism. But at least
they were honest about the 'crime' attributed to me. I was sentenced then, with the friends I mentioned in the letter....I asked
the Party for action of solidarity with these imprisoned friends,
and called also on Israeli workers and supporters of peace to

express solidarity. It never occurred that such a letter could
endanger security. In 1973 I was interviewed by Eric Rouleau
for Le Monde, and in it I specially stated the Jordanian Communist Party's stand in favour of Israeli self-determination and
negotiations with Israel. I also said that for 26 years my
friends and I have claimed the right of the establishing of a
Palestinian state alongside Israel. All that while Arab reaction-
aries called us 'traitors'....My purpose in the letter was to
protest at the attack on the Communist Party - arrests and pressure on my friends - and to call for solidarity."

He continued, "If the authorities see the letter as espionage, I feel that the forces of peace and democracy in Israel will
understand in their hearts, and that is what I want most. I was
accused of spying to cover up the political oppression of Communists, an old and dishonest game, and, sadly, it was a Jew who
first fell victim to it. He was defended by Emile Zola, and I am
sure that there will be an Emile Zola in Israel too."

At this point the judge intervened, "You talk of Emile Zola
in a military court !"

Bashir answered, "Emile Zola symbolized the conscience
of the people, the conscience of people everywhere." He concluded,
"I am against occupation and will continue to struggle against it."

There was no shortage of tension. I was still influenced
by Muhammad Yasin's sentence, given by the same president.
I also recalled Colonel Gershon Orion's unfavourable response to
my appeal. He blazed with anger and warned me that I would be
charged with contempt of court if I continued. He also warned
Nikara of the same thing.

The prosecution summed up its case and recommended
that Bashir be found guilty.

It had grown dark outside as I began my summary.
"There is no espionage, no spy. A member of a political party
was heard in court today - a man seeking to make contact with
his party on the East Bank by the only way open to him, by letter."
I tried to show that there had been no element of espionage,

quoting from Ha-Derech information similar to the contents of the
letter. I pointed out that I had reported on the arrests in a press
conference in London on 15 May 1974, and that this had appeared
in the British press. "If what Bashir has done is espionage, then
we are all spies."

During my speech the lights failed, and the judges asked
for an adjournment. My suggestion that I finish by gaslamp was
rejected.

The third session took place on 12 February. The cold of
the police station was offset by the crowd of Bashir's relatives and
Jewish friends, who packed the room. Among them were M Vilner,
Secretary General of the Israeli Communist Party, and R Luvitch,
member of the political bureau.

The lawyers were Nikara, A Hafiz Darawsha, W Fahum,
L Tzemel, S al-Haj and A Adamat.

I continued my summary and dealt with the names mentioned in the letter. If they were confidential, the censor could
have stopped them. As for his desire to call on his friends for
solidarity, he was not alone – many public figures and organizations
in Israel and outside had protested at the administrative arrests.
I cited a list of names, professors, writers, Knesset members of
different parties; I quoted Knesset member M Vilner, "peace interests
demand that the administrative prisoners be released". The memorandum of the League of Human and Civil Rights noted that these
arrests "hurt the image of the state. Bashir had called for an
appeal to Israeli public opinion, to Israeli workers – should he
therefore be accused of espionage ? With the same logic, those
who demonstrated against the arrests were spies as well.

I refuted the claim that the letter endangered the security
of the state. I pointed out that Bashir was a member of the political bureau of the Jordanian Communist Party, and that his letter
was for his friend Dr Ziadin of the same organization. Ziadin,
a member of Parliament when the Nabulsi Government was in
office, had also been called a 'traitor' for his stand in favour of
the recognition of Israel.

I objected that the Shin Beit 'expert' brought by the prosecution had not answered most of my questions, and I quoted British sources about such prejudiced 'experts'. However, I said, at least he had mentioned that the National Palestinian Front had supported the Security Council's decision on the solution of the conflict.

His innocence was also proved by the fact that Salah Abd al-Al (later to be tried in Nablus under the same judge) on whom the letter was found, has not been accused of passing it on, but of a completely different offence.

Here sits a Communist, I said, but no-one has the courage to accuse him of that. Only under fascist regimes do Communists go to jail for their opinions. If Barguti is convicted it will do disservice to our people. We cannot strike off the hand stretched out towards us. Bashur must be acquitted of all blame.

There was much tension as Nikara told how a friend had asked him why such a veteran lawyer was appearing in military court on a case where the sentence had already been decided. Usually....

Judge Orion jumped from his seat red with anger, to announce that the bench was going out to make their decision. After a long time they returned to announce that Nikara's words sounded like contempt, but that the case would be heard out before the decision would be made.

Nikara continued. He had told his friend, "It is my job to defend my client before the court for two reasons, because the trial is political and I believe my client is innocent, and because his freedom is at stake. I did not intend to insult the court."

The judges remarked that the second part of his statement did not excuse the first, but that they had faith in his sincerity. He continued his summary for the defence.

"We feel that this it a first-class political trial."

The judge: "The military court does not deal with politics."

Nikara: "We claim that the defendant is innocent. These are facts and we ask that the trial be based on them. The accused

has said how he wrote the letter quickly to take advantage of someone to pass it on. Thus he did not plan it in advance. How can the
prosecutor accuse him of 'gathering, copying down, possessing
and transmitting information' ? Does a letter from a member
of the political bureau of a Communist organization to a colleague
describing arrests, asking if students should be sent to study,
and if women could be sent to a conference, a letter asking for
guidance, need to be brought to court ? Where is the criminal
intent to harm the security of the area ? It is an internal matter
for the Party."

Nikara refuted the claim that the National Palestinian
Front was an arm of the Jordanian Communist Party. The 'expert'
had claimed that Dr Ziadin had a clinic to which members of other
organizations came. But every political party communicates with
others, just as Begin can meet Rabin.

Nikara quoted al-Itihad which had published the names
mentioned in Barguti's letter. He pointed out that Barguti had
arrived in the West Bank on 26 March 1974 and sent the letter on
2 May. He was arrested on 30 June, so that for three months no
evidence had been found against him to bring a criminal charge.

Darawsha, speaking in favour of acquittal, was listened to
intently.

"It is an historical error to put a Palestinian leader on
trial, when, almost certainly, tomorrow he will be among those
we will sit with to negotiate peace." He recalled that King Hussein
had sentenced him for being a Communist who favoured recognition
of Israel and the carrying out of UN decisions in the Middle East.
He said that the trial was another in a series of incitements against
the Communist Party, and that the court must contribute to justice.
He must be acquitted in the interests of relations between the two
peoples in the future.

The lawyer Leah Tzemel asked to express her hope that
Barguti would be acquitted, believing that conviction would lead
to charges against many others. She pointed to the responsibility
of the court in making a just decision.

The 27th February was the day of the decision. There was great tension. Bashir's wife's face expressed concern as she sat with her family to listen.

Many came to hear the decision, including members of the Israeli Communist Party and the Palestinian Communist Party. Among the audience were Knesset members Tawfiq Toubi, Tawfiq Ziad, Wolf Erlich, chairperson of the Central Committee of Inquiries, Hans Lebrecht, member of the Central Committee, and Yehuda Unger, also a member, the Chief Editor of <u>Zu Ha-Derech</u>, and others. A delegation from the Israeli League of Human and Civil Rights headed by the author Mordecai Avi-Shaul also came. The trial was widely covered by the press, radio and television.

The military governor of Ramallah refused permission to attend to many people, including Israeli youths. His arrogance got him into an argument with Professor Daniel Amit, who also wanted to attend. Tawfiq Ziad was forced to stand outside for half an hour for permission to enter.

President Gershon Orion read out the decision. The atmosphere in the room was disturbed only by flashes from the television cameras and the movements of the photographers.

The decision accepted the defence claim that there was no justification in putting Bashir on trial.

The judges decided that he could not be charged with spying as claimed by the prosecution, that he had committed no transgression whatever and had no intention of doing so. "The appearance of the accused in court was honourable and correct, and I believe the sincerity of his words. I believe that all his activities, including the writing of the letter, were undertaken within the framework of his party. His concern was for his detained and tortured friends," said the judge.

He rejected the prosecution's evidence based only on the Shin Beit 'expert', and refuted Major M Farkush's claim that the letter was harmful to the 'security of the area'. If it was harmful, why had the prosecutor agreed to its publication in the press ?

In the part of the decision dealing with the legal analysis
of the accusations of collecting information and harming the
security of the area, the judge fully accepted the prosecution's
claims.

Thus Bashir was acquitted. Joy prevailed, and there
were hugs, kisses and applause. I too shared the mood of
rejoicing. After many months, Bashir could return to his house
and his children.

I accompanied him to jail to conclude the formal process
of his release. I wanted us to leave the jail together; it is something,
which, for me, is symbolic. Unfortunately, it happens very rarely.

We all went to Bashir's family house. Glasses were raised,
greetings exchanged. Bashir thanked all who had stood by him.
Laila Najab was present. I raised my glass to the women, the wives
of the prisoners who were still in jail, and whose sentences had
been extended another six months, women fighting for the release
of their husbands.

Bashir came with us to the car, our first handshake outside the walls. Our eyes met, and I knew he was thinking of his
friends still inside.

On the same day Lotfi Zarih, a veteran Communist from
Jaffa, became the father of a boy. On his way to hospital he heard
on an Israeli broadcast that Bashir had been acquitted and released.
Thus one Bashir was released and another born. Bashir Zarih is
now almost a year old. If only the day would come when courts and
prisons no longer hold those fighting for the freedom of their people.

EXPULSION

There was widespread joy at Bashir's release. Friends called

to congratulate me on the success, and I thought that it might
teach our leaders that this was not the way to act.

And so they understood....

These were the days of hunger strikes in the prisons
against the renewal of administrative arrests. I arranged to
visit Suliman, who had been in solitary confinement in Ramla
prison for about the last nine months. I had decided on this in
Bashir's house as the glasses were raised, and I had seen the
eyes of his wife Laila.

I visited him every so often in Ramla, and each visit
brought us closer together. He told me that my visit to Ramallah
after his arrest had saved his life. The Shin Beit, who had arrested him in the street, had told him that now they had him to
themselves and that no-one knew of his arrest, and that his choice
was to talk or die. Hence their anger with me. But he had understood that his life had been saved. More than once he told me
that in the most difficult days he had felt that their hands were tied,
that they feared that he would die. "For this, my friends, I thank
those with consciences in Israel and the world, and those of my
own people who struggle."

He spent his days reading, though at first this was not
allowed. He told me that during our visit to Jamleh on 2 July,
he had twisted his neck painfully after being beaten. He had got
used to the position when they beat him.

One thing frightened him more than anything: expulsion.
"I am willing to undergo any suffering, but only in my homeland,
I am not afraid of prison, but I want to feel the soil of my home-
land under my feet."

When I came to the prison on 28 February 1975, I was
going to tell him about Bashir's trial. I knew he would be happy,
for I knew of his concern for his friends.

Later on, I was unable to see him in prison. I was
afraid he would be tortured again, or that he was about to suffer
the expulsion he feared so much.

The race against time began in my office: I had met

a large crowd of Israeli women demonstrating solidarity with the
families of prisoners who were holding a sit-in strike at the
Red Cross office in East Jerusalem.

We submitted a request for an order nisi, and received it.
I telephoned the Ministry of Defence and told them I had an order
forbidding the expulsion of Suliman. I did not know that he was
already in Lebanon, with his fellow administrative prisoners
Abdallah al-Siryani and Mahmud Shukair. This news came half an
hour later.

I went with Laila to the Red Cross office. Terror and anger
struck the women. I spoke to them of the authorities' crime, the
additional crime that everyone with a conscience abhorred. The
Jewish and Arab friends from Israel stayed with the striking women.
I went home feeling as if I had been orphaned. Laila's eyes followed me, as did Suliman's words, "Anything is better than expulsion."

Late that night I wrote him a letter. I knew it would
reach him, and here it is:

To Suliman al-Najab
We could not part as friends properly do. In our last conversation we talked of everything and the guards were astonished:
what are they discussing for so long ? "This will be the last
occupation in the world", you said to me then. I wrote down
your words so that they could be quoted, and you scolded me
for doing so. But your words now have wings because of their
burning truth from within prison walls.

When I got to the prison yesterday they told me you weren't
there. The officer on duty said, "The soldiers took him away."
I was startled, because more than once in the past soldiers
have taken you 'somewhere' to torture you again and again,
till they found they had never met anyone as tough as you. The
man, seeing my surprise, asked me, "What are you so excited
about ? Does he owe you money ?" Then it was the administration's turn. Of course, they had 'no idea' where you had
been taken, or what was to be your fate. The fear that they

had expelled you gripped me, for over the last months I had
come to realise how important the soil of your homeland was
to you. As your little daughter said, 'My father is in jail because he loves his homeland.' Your torturers knew this well,
Suliman. They knew this love was your strength. When your
body was bleeding and you were dazed with blows, this love
guarded your proud spirit. For nine months you were held in
solitary confinement. How they feared your ideas of peace.
They confined you behind steel doors, but the truth about you
and your heroism reached other prisons and young and old
told legends of you. I know your modesty, and that you will
protest at my saying such things, but as a revolutionary you
should be pleased that your torture was not in vain, and that a
new generation of fighters for justice and peace will be
brought up in the light of your example.

Again I recall that day in Ramallah prison, April 30, when
I saw you facing the wall. You turned and our eyes met. They
took me away, angry that they had failed to conceal your whereabouts.

And the other visits, when you were weak from torture; the
one in Jamleh when I saw your wound. Your wife Laila and
sister Rukieh waited outside, and I feared they would read in
my eyes what I had seen. They cross-examined me, and I
couldn't hide anything from them for you were before my eyes
the whole time.

Then there were other visits, and the friendship and solidarity between us grew stronger.

More than once you sent greetings and thanks to the forces
in Israel who rose against the oppression and humiliation of
your people.

I tried to prevent your expulsion. Laila was with me all
through that morning, and there was a moment when it seemed
as if we might succeed. But it was not to be. When Laila
realised you were no longer here, she went pale, and friends
rushed to support her; but she didn't need them, and went to

encourage other women instead, with a smile on her face.
That is Laila.

It is time to end this letter, to leave something for us to
talk about in the days to come when you return home - with
the ending of the last occupation. Till then, accept greetings,
my friend Suliman, from Jews and Arabs who detest oppression and call for a genuine peace.
In friendship,
Felicia Langer, 1 March 1975

Mahmud Shukair, writer and teacher, had endured administrative
detention for over a year since 1969[1]. This time when Mahmud,
a man in poor health, was arrested it was made certain that he
would not be ill-treated. His father came to my office, very
worried about his son's fate, but I knew that the investigators
feared to hurt him because any injury could be dangerous. On 5
August 1974 I saw him in the solitary confinement section at
Jamleh. He had not been beaten, but had been threatened that he
would be tortured if his case appeared in al-Itihad, al-Fajar or
al-Shaab.

He was liked by everyone in Kfar Yona prison, where he
was held with other prisoners from East Jerusalem. He had received a prize for the best story written in Jordan. His life was
dedicated to the fight for justice for his people and he strove for
a just peace and for the co-existence of the two peoples. And this in
the most difficult moments.

Abdallah Siryani was arrested on 23 December 1973 in
the street, and the Shin Beit told him that now he was in their
hands they could do as they liked with him.

His family and I were told of his arrest only a month and
a half later, and his place of detention. When I came to Ramallah,
even though the most difficult time was over, he told me what he

---

1. A description of this is found in With My Own Eyes

had undergone, and his voice shook. At night they had tied him to
the door naked, his hands behind him, and sprayed him with water.
On snowy nights he was taken outside, and snow put on his feet and
under his arm-pits. 'You held demonstrations against the occupation.
You printed al-Watan ' they accused him. He denied it, and they
threatened to kill him. He replied that it wouldn't change anything;
he would be one of thousands of war victims. For days he had no
sleep. His exposure to the cold clad only in underclothes was an
amusement for his investigators, Abu Hanni and Abu Jamil. At
their failure, they threatened to tell his party he was a traitor so
as to get him expelled. They gave him no water, and no opportunity
to wash.

But he remained silent, telling them only, "What I am
doing is for the good of my people and yours, what you are doing
is against the good of both."

Abdallah's detention was extended several times, and
eventually he was expelled with Suliman and Mahmud. The expulsion
was carried out secretly, so that no-one could help or appeal to
the High Court of Justice or Committee of Appeals.

APPEAL

As I wrote those lines about Abdallah, I remembered a session
of the Committee of Appeals against administrative arrests. The
Committee, almost without authority, would never tell the accused
or his lawyer what the charge was.

The detainees, realising the uselessness of the institution,
usually boycotted its proceedings.

But in the beginning we tried this dubious resource as well, and here is an account of one session, held on 14 April.

The Committee met in the Director's room at Ramallah prison, and consisted of three judges of whom one, the chairman, has legal experience. Shin Beit officials arrive from Ramallah, Hebron and Nablus, and prisoners likewise.

The first prisoner appeared without a lawyer, requesting his release, not knowing why he has been arrested. The chairman takes notes. "We will let you know the decision later," he tells the prisoner, who doesn't understand that this is the end of the discussion. He was led from the room to a cell.

The second is Abdallah Siryani. I speak for him. "It is extremely difficult for me to appear when the Shin Beit here have information about Abdallah which I am forbidden to know." Two committee members look surprised, as they were not aware that all information should be restricted, and that when the Shin Beit made their accusations against prisoners, both lawyers and prisoners had to leave the room.

Chairman: "Madam, understand us. An administrative prisoner in Gaza was once freed, on the recommendation of the local government. They said he was a friend of the Governor. Soon after, he was caught throwing a grenade in Gaza. You can imagine the feelings of the members of the committee who released him."

"In your shoes I would always be wary of those who co-operated. Abdallah does not. He has not made friends with the Governor; quite the contrary. He is openly opposed to occupation. He favours a peaceful solution, recognizes the right of Israel to exist, but he will not concede the rights of Palestinians. If that is a transgression, why don't you say so plainly ?"

The next was Adel Barguti from Kfar Kovar. He has been given a year's detention, and has also been held in Jafar prison in Jordan for about seven years. I remarked, "It looks as though you are using King Hussein's lists, and I don't think that is much to our credit."

Barguti states, "The Shin Beit came to my cell and asked

if I would negotiate with them in the name of the 'National Front in the West Bank'. I said I did not belong to it and was not able to speak for it." It was obvious from this that the 'diplomats' of the Shin Beit had failed to draw him out in prison. He also refused to co-operate with them. He, also, requested to be released.

Muhammad Saada of Hebron appears. He, too, was one of King Hussein's clients at Jafar in the past. "I am a chicken merchant," he says, "What do they want from me ? The Shin Beit told me that as a merchant I must understand the business of buying and selling: I would sell to them and they would set me free. He told me that he wanted me to co-operate with them. I refused. I want to go on being a chicken merchant."

There are sixteen people in his family. Twelve children. Saada finishes speaking, and is taken out.

The last prisoner is young Bassem Amira. He has suffered great torture, and an appeal was made to the High Court of Appeals because the authorities had refused to allow his parents and lawyer to see him. He was accused of throwing a grenade at the military governor's car. He had an alibi. The torture didn't help; Bassem confessed nothing. As punishment he was sentenced to a year's detention. With great force Bassem protested at his arrest and demanded to be freed or brought to trial.

The meeting is over. The Shin Beit will now have their say about the arrests, but without the prisoners present. They will have no idea of what is being attributed to them.

I will return later to a session of the Committee in Hebron prison, the last in which I appeared.

Other prisoners from Ramallah also appeared, among them the following:

Taisir al-Agugi, a graduate of a Soviet university. We spoke several times together, sometimes in Russian, and I found him highly educated. Ghassan al-Harb is also a Soviet graduate. His wife, Afaf, had a son while he was in prison. Adnan Dagar is that his arrest was really an attempt by the authorities to break that his arrest was really an attemp by the authorities to break the trade unions. Hadar al-Alam had known Hussein's prisons, and experienced Israeli detention more than once.

Prisoners from Kfar Yona, such as Yakoub Farah, a permanent inmate of the prison, Faruh Salfiti, likewise, and Halil Toma, whose poems written in jail are so popular; all sent greetings to the progressive forces in Israel, to the League of Human and Civil Rights, and to the newspapers al-Figari and al-Shaab.

Their arrest only strengthened their belief that their way was the right one.

A ROOF OVER ONE'S HEAD

Azam al-Aklik sits before me. The cold of Nablus jail numbs the bones. There is a fresh scar on his forehead. Two fingers on his left hand have been amputated, and part of his palm has no feeling. He tells of the hardships of his investigation, after he was wounded handling explosives. He was taken to hospital and beaten even before he received medical treatment. Azam goes over the names of the investigators; all known from the years of the occupation.

He is twenty-two. He married his wife Laila nine months ago, and she is now expecting a baby.

"Did you see my family house ?" he asks me, then correcting himself, "or rather, what's left of it.....it's not far from the jail so you could go and see it."

Walid goes with me. He asks passers-by where it is, and a few look at him suspiciously.

We arrive. The ruins can be seen from afar. The front door is blocked. Below, in the small basement, signs of life can still be seen - sheets hanging out. We go down the steep hill.

Window grills, blocks of stone and rubble. The walls stand out in green - newly painted. Suddenly I sense the full meaning of the phrase 'a roof over one's head.'

Azam's wife and mother greet us and invite us into the narrow room. The mother begins, "Azam was arrested in October, when he was wounded. We feared for him. Two months later I dreamt that they came here, threw us out and destroyed the house. That was the day they really came, the soldiers. The surrounded the house, and the Governor of Nablus was there. They gave us half an hour to get our things out, half an hour to collect everything we have gathered in a lifetime. There are fifteen of us - do you understand ? And the children, what will become of them ? The neighbours helped us to get things together, and what we didn't have time to remove, was destroyed. How did they destroy it, you ask ? Explosives were not enough; it was well-built, we had built it two years ago. They brought a bulldozer as well, and they worked very hard. They told us to throw her, his pregnant wife, into the street as well. She went, and returned again to this small room."

Laila turned to me, interrupting the mother to ask about Azam. I answer, and the mother continues. "We divided the children between the relatives." She shows us photographs. Smiling faces, a table set for a celebration, a wide room, decorated walls. A shelter that is no more.

We go out to the yard. It is raining and a strong wind is blowing. Azam's mother remembers, "A lot of the household things got wet. It was December, cold and rainy, and the things stayed outside for several days."

We part. The neighbour's children look at me, their eyes searching, the same eyes that not long ago saw the destruction of the house.

Nablus, the end of January 1975. A hill facing us in green tranquillity, and under our feet a volcano.

Azam, who caused harm to himself alone, is sentenced to life imprisonment by the military court. President of the Panel, Colonel Gershon Orion, read the decision smiling. Among the audience is Azam's wife, with a baby born while the father was in prison.

THE DECEIT

As I have said, we decided to boycott the Committee of Appeals. The last one we attended was that held in Hebron on Thursday 7 April at the prison. The judges, prosecutor and Shin Beit all assembled on the appointed day, and one by one the prisoners were brought. Halil Rasmawi, a teacher in Bethlehem University a graduate from a Soviet university; Atallah, a leader of workers; Abd al-Majid Hamdan, a teacher in Bethlehem, father of our sick friend Muhammad Saada; Daud Mashar. A procession of people expressing their views and their faith in their people and desire for peace. Someone remarks, "This is like the Geneva Conference !" "True. but the other side, willing to speak to you, is imprisoned,"I reply.

One of the last is Husni Hadad. I point out, since the session is coming to an end, that we shall not appear again, and that we refuse to be a tool for the authorities in giving the impression that there is redress for administrative detention.

The truth, as we know, is that the remedy is not in the hands of the Committee, but in those of the Shin Beit.

"But,nevertheless, you appeared this time," remarks the judge. "Yes. We wanted to give you a last chance. If we succeed today, we will change our decision."

Husni shows the marks of torture. The judge says that this does not interest him. The Shin Beit man said that the appeal I had submitted to the High Court of Appeals had ensured that the police investigating committee had acted fairly, and that there had been no torture. Thus the matter of torture was closed.

"Maybe as far as you and the High Court are concerned, the matter is closed, but where we are concerned, it is not. Neither here nor abroad has this chapter come to an end."

The meeting finished in the afternoon. The prisoners greet me as I leave. As always wishes for success. "Next time we shall meet at home," - and my heart is full of hope that perhaps this might happen.

The next evening, Friday, I receive a call from a friend in East Jerusalem. "We have just heard that Husni Hadad, Halil Hajazi, Hussein Abu Jarbieh and two others from Gaza - Othman al-Afi and Abed Zouhiri - have been expelled to Lebanon." I felt stupified, especially over Husni, who had appeared only yesterday before the Committee. I checked, and found it was true according to Arab radio stations. On the Saturday it was announced on Israeli stations.

I could not help thinking of Husni before the Committee in the presence of the Shin Beit, who had listened to him patiently while the expulsion order was already in their possession. After we had left, as I was told later, Husni was taken to an unknown place. His appearance was simply a deception. If I had suspected anything I could have produced a conditional order at once stopping the expulsion, at least temporarily. But I was so concerned with realizing our 'democratic right' to appeal against the detention. The show was so perfect, the attention paid to what Husni had to say so complete, with no clues to suggest that everything was ordered and ready and that they were just waiting for me to leave.

The lesson was most instructive. The families appeared as if in mourning. Hussein Abu Garbieh's wife looked like a ghost. Hussein, as a young man, had been in and out of jail on administrative detention. He married, set up house, then all was destroyed. Halil Hajazi's wife, who had feared for his life throughout his investigation, remained in Nablus in a state of shock.

Relatives of those still in prison came to my office, brought by the fear of expulsion. We decided to submit a collective appeal to the High Court and demand an order against expulsion.

I prepared a request for 28 prisoners in the name of members of their families.

I pointed out in the plea that all of them had been threatened with expulsion by the Shin Beit in the past. The expulsion of Husni Hadad, done so deceitfully under cover of his appearance before the Committee, showed the bad faith of the Minister of Defence. The authorities were determined to solve the problem of the arrests by expelling the prisoners from their homeland. I described how the expulsion had been carried out, with no chance of appeal to any judicial body. The Defence Regulation (Emergency Act) of 1945, which governs expulsion, provided for a respite to enable the deportee to take his case to appeal as a last resort. I attached to the plea the documents concerning Suliman al-Najab and described how we had been deceived.

It was late, after two o'clock in the afternoon, and all the judges had left. In accordance to my request I was referred to Judge H Cohen's house. The secretary pressed speed on me so that I could return by three to have the order typed, so that I could submit it. An order becomes valid only when certified. I also requested an order against the Minister of Defence, responsible for the expulsion.

Salah and I went to Judge Cohen's house. He opened the door himself and I explained why the matter was urgent. In his study he examined my plea. Salah and I held our breath as we followed his expression. I sensed that if I failed this time, they would be able to treat prisoners as they liked.

After a few questions, Judge Cohen agreed to give me an injunction ordering that the other petitioners should not be expelled beyond Israel's borders, or land held by her, until a decision had been made about the plea.

We felt great relief. This time there was a lot in the press about the injunction order, saying that though it was only temporary assistance, it still marked a great success. The discussion of the plea was fixed for a month later.

On the day the room was crowded with relatives of detainees. Before I could speak, the President, Y Sussman, confronted
me: "What is your plea actually based on ? Did the Minister of
Defence tell you he planned to expel them ?" "He did not tell me
anything," I replied, "neither to me nor my clients. He simply
expelled them in the middle of the night, as I have said in my plea."
The judges, "In that case, is it possible to submit a plea in the
name of three million residents of Israel, in danger of expulsion
for no concrete reason ?" I answer, "My clients are not three
million residents of Israel. They are being detained without charge
or trial, and have been threatened by the authorities with expulsion
on different occasions. Their friends have been expelled in the
way I have described. What more concrete reasons do I need ?
If I wait any longer I will find them tomorrow in Beirut or Amman.
When the British were here they expelled people to their colonies.
Are Lebanon and Jordan our colonies ? "

Judge Sussman is intransigent. "You like coming here to
bother us, Ms Langer" he remarks jeeringly. "How could I like
coming here when I am treated like this ?" I reply, "But is there
anywhere else I could go where human rights are violated so
crudely ?"

"Until you appeal to the Minister of Defence to ask if he
has any intention of expelling the persons mentioned in the petition
we will not hear your request, which, to our regret, has no basis."

I asked them to at least extend the period of the restraining
order, and took upon myself to appeal to the Minister of Defence
to reveal his intentions. Those intentions, which were clear to
everyone but the judges.

The order was extended for another fifteen days. In my
request to the Minister I asked him to indicate if his intentions
were to expel the persons 'at any time' and to give a clear and
unambiguous answer.

In his answer he stated that he had no intention at present
to expel them, but he pointed out that "any action taken in the past,
or to be taken in the future by the authorized authorities was done

and will be done in accordance with the law and as the law dictates."

Again a meeting was fixed in the Supreme Court. Judge Sussman read the letter and said, "What else do you want ? The authorities do not intend to expell them, and if they do, it will be done legally. Nothing can be done here in the court."

I again described how the others had been expelled, pointing out that it had not been done legally, and thus there was no truth in the Minister's words that in the past he had acted in accordance with the law. I took out the Defence Regulations and cited that of 1947, that anyone given an expulsion order had the right to appear before a committee of appeal, and to appeal against the order. "How could they have appealed with their hands tied, their eyes blindfolded, taken straight from the prisons to the Lebanese border, to the security fence, and told, 'If you return we will shoot you'..."

The judges asked for the updated regulations and came to the conclusion that I was right.

I ask that the court at least point to and confirm that such is the right of the petitioners, in the event of their being expelled. Sussman tells me that this is not a matter for the court. The Minister has promised to act in accordance with the law, and that is enough. I sensed I was going to lose, for they clearly wanted to give the Minister a free hand.

I appealed to the judges again, as a last request: that what the law says be pointed out. "You are the petitioners' last resort !"

They take counsel and decide to reject the plea in the light of the Minister's promise. But in their order, Sussman writes, "Whoever is served with an expulsion order has the right to appeal to a special committee set up according to regulation 112(8). Having studied the appeal, the committee will submit its recommendations to the government, who will make a final decision."

Thus, although the plea was rejected, the goal was attained. I t had been determined that no-one could be expelled from

his homeland without being given a chance to appeal against the
order, something that had not occurred till now.

Clearly, the authorities would be reluctant to carry out
expulsions if they aroused public opinion, and if the accused had
the chance to be heard and to explain to everyone the criminal nature of the expulsion.

THE GOLAN HEIGHTS

17 April 1975 and the anniversary of the independence of Syria
from French rule. That day, in three villages, Majdal Shams,
Bokata and Masada, Syrian national flags were raised on school
roof-tops. There was no limit to the anger and irritation from
the military authorities. Searches were made in all three villages.

The first house belonged to a Golan Heights leader, but
nothing was found. His young son, Faras, was arrested, beaten
and then released. Young Salim Hatar was also arrested and
bady beaten, and returned to his house black and blue and in need
of medical help.

The authorities were incensed because the flags flew for
twenty-four hours, seen by all, though no-one saw fit to report
the 'crime' to the authorities. In revenge, police beat children
in the area without mercy or discrimination. They also took a
new step: they arrested a young Druze woman, Amira Abu Jabal,
aged sixteen. Her brother is Azat Abu Jabal, who had been killed
three years before by Israeli guards as he tried to cross into Syria.
Her father, Shahiv Abu Jabal, had been sentenced to thirty years
in prison, and her brother Yousif to fifteen. She was freed after
investigation, having spent one night in prison at Kiriat Smona.

In connection with the flag affair, three people were arrested from Majdal Shams, Nazia Ibrahim, Nazia Abu Jabal, and Raniz al-Tzafadi, and three from Bokata: Mahmud Salman Amsha Salman Jabar Ahbus and Izat Salim Shams.

A week later I went to Majdal Shams and talked with young and old. "Why are you so afraid of the flag, and why take your anger out on children in the streets ?   It doesn't show much strength or self-confidence."

BEATING AND TORTURE

Recently, the League for Human and Civil Rights called for the immediate cessation of investigations that included beating and torture.

In a memorandum from the League, newspaper reports were quoted to testify to the violence used by the police, as in the case of Mitzner, accused of murdering the owner of a pastry shop. His police station confession was cancelled when, after a medical check had been allowed by the judge, it was found that it had been forced from him by beatings and torture.

The memorandum pointed out that both military and civil courts normally rejected claims of torture during detention and investigation.

"We call on the Israeli police", it said, "in the light of other recent rulings in connection with beatings, and especially after the ruling of the court of Jaffa-Tel Aviv in the case of Mitzner. This disgrace must be stopped, and the principle must be respected that every person is innocent until proved guilty, that punishment cannot be given without a sentence, and that no punishment not prescribed by law can be given. It is not enough to transfer those responsible to other positions. Every policeman and officer must realise his responsibility for the abuse of prisoners." Since publication of this proclamation, many judges in civil courts across the country have determined that prisoners have been beaten and tortured, and the police have been censured.

But in dozens of military courts and in many hundreds of cases concerning Arabs from the occupied territories, complaints of beating and torture are rejected daily, and continue to be rejected daily.

Marks of violence on prisoners' bodies fail to convince judges. Fellow prisoners who have witnessed the beatings have been described as liars over the eight years of trials since the occupation began. I have seen it myself over many years.

Not once was it found that the investigation had been carried out illegally, or that violence had been used. The wounds shown to the judge are not wounds, and their evidence sworn on the Koran or the New Testament is always a lie.

Thus, there is one kind of prisoner for whom any kind of investigation is legal - the Arabs.

IHSAN

I met Ihsan many times, and remember him standing before the steel gate of Jamele prison at the beginning of 1973. His brother Ahmad from Majdal Shams, and many other sons of the Golan Heights, were held in that prison. He stood there waiting anxiously, his face like that of a young boy.

Ihsan is specially disliked by the occupation authorities; not only can he not come to terms with it, but he wants to study,

to succeed, and likes to think that others of his generation will do
the same. The edict covering the children of the Golan Heights
is harsh: unlike their counterparts in the West Bank and Gaza
Strip who are allowed to study in institutions in Arab countries,
the people of the Golan Heights are limited to their villages, and
are thus prohibited higher education. Ihsan was among those
who worked to get the edict changed, appealing to all the institutions
involved. But all appeals were rejected.

He was arrested four times in succession, investigated,
badly beaten, and freed.

He decided to study in the Technion, and reached the
third year in the department of agriculture.

But then, on 20 April 1975, he was arrested from the
dormitories and taken at once to Akko prison to solitary confinement.

This time his investigator was Abu Hanni, who told him
that this time they would be very thorough, as they expected to
have him as a guest for a long time. Their questions were many
and varied. Even his activities at school came up, including his
objections to the Israeli curriculum, demonstrations against the
Balfour Declaration, his celebration of Palestine Day and Syrian
Independence, circulating of proclamations and burning of the
Israeli flag. Ihsan also remembered his first arrest, when pupils
from his school went with the mukhtar to the military governor
saying that they would not return to school till Ihsan was freed.

The investigator omitted nothing, reminding Ihsan of
his objection to the hanging of pictures of Israeli politicians on
school walls. Abu Hanni showed his concern for those who co-
operated with the military government of the Heights, questioning
Ihsan about the threatening letters sent to them.

Ihsan's articles in al-Itihad and al-Jedid, translations of
those written by progressive Israelis, and his relations with other
progressives were also subjects of investigation. Abu Hanni
was specially concerned with his translation of Israel Shahak's
book, Zionism – The Whole Truth, chapters of which were pub-

lished in al-Jedid. A visit to Ihsan by the poet Samih al-Qasem
aroused anger. Ihsan had invited others to hear the poems, and
they also sang patriotic Syrian songs. But Abu Hanni was angry
most of all at Ihsan's activities among the university students
and within the Student Council, together with his political views.
He was also tested with a lie detector. He was questioned
closely about his brother Ahmad, who had been sentenced to four
years, of whom he was proud.

He was held twenty-six days in solitary confinement
while the investigators tried to make him confess to spying for
Syrian Intelligence, without success. He wrote slogans on the
walls and doors, patriotic poetry, and poems of proletarian inter-
nationalism. On May Day he hung out a flag he had made from his
vest. The guards beat him for this, but he celebrated May Day in
his heart.

Thus it was inside the prison; outside all was not quiet.
His fellow students continued vigorous activity in solidarity,
aimed at his release. Thousands of proclamations were distributed telling of the oppression of university students involved in
political activity, including at the grave of the Nabi Shuaib at the
annual pilgrimage on 25 April 1975. This aroused the anger of
thousands of Druze visitors there that day, and the matter became
a public political issue thanks to the initiative of the Druze
Council. Slogans "Free political prisoners - free Ihsan Kadmani !"
appeared on the walls of the Technion; erased in the evening, they
would be there again next morning.

The Union of Arab Students called for a public meeting
supporting the release of political prisoners and of Ihsan. Thousands came, and clashed with the right-wing. Letters protesting
at his detention appeared in the student press, and were sent to
the Dean of the Technion asking for his support for Ihsan. The
Communist newspaper al-Shaab devoted much space to his arrest,
demanding his release. Professor Shahak appealed to human rights
organizations abroad and to the Israeli Government, demanding
his freedom. Communist MPs and MP Marsha Friedman sub-

mitted questions about his detention. The affair aroused opinion
abroad as well, and the linguist Noam Chomsky, from the Massa-
chusetts Institute of Technology, sent a letter of solidarity to
Ihsan.

In prison, cut off though he was, Ihsan sensed something
was happening. He was no longer beaten. The Shin Beit had
failed. There was no alternative but to free him, and he was
released after a month in prison.

But an order of banishment to his village was placed on
him, and another to report to the police. This remained in effect
till after the beginning of the academic year at the Technion, in
the hope that he would not be able to continue his studies.

But university life opened its arms to him, and he was
to pass all its tests.

HELSINKI

After many failures in proving that torture took place during investigations and that other violations of human rights existed in
the occupied territories, I had said more than once that I would
be willing to appear before any international forum to give evidence of what my eyes had seen and of what I knew through my
work as an attorney for prisoners of the occupation.

I knew that the World Council for Peace had set up a
committee to look into the violation of human rights in Israel
and the lands it had occupied in June 1967. It first met in Beirut
and many witnesses appeared before it. Its second meeting was
in May 1975 in Helsinki to hear additional testimony, and I was
invited to appear. Three of us went, Avi-Shaul, Hanna Nikara

and myself. For a moment I forgot that the meeting was far from a homeland to which they could not return.

The committee comprised Romish Shandra, Secretary-General of the World Council for Peace; A B M Kamra, Minister of Information and Communications in Sierra Leone- Leo Keohatla, member of the Finnish Parliament, of the Social Democratic Party; Olag Goyanov, legal expert from the USSR; A Rinini, member of the Italian Christian Democrat Party; and R Batiah, member of the Indian Parliament and representative of the Congress Party.

Meetings took place in Finland Hall, afterwards used for the European Summit, and were widely covered by the Finnish press. Suliman's testimony took me back to the days of his detention. Many had tears in their eyes, and I saw him chained to the door of his cell, the floor covered with sharp stones. Perhaps a committee like this one might meet at the Beit Solokov (press centre) in Tel Aviv one day, with the press, and ask him questions, and go with him to the places he was describing.

Mahmud Shukair told of the oppression of educated Arabs, the interference with the Arab school curriculum designed to obliterate the national identity of those in the West Bank. He also told of his own bitter experience, twice in detention, before his expulsion.

Dr Mustafa Milhem spoke of the expropriation of Arab land, the destruction of houses and expulsions of Palestinians during the occupation, giving figures to support his arguments. He spoke at length of the illegal activities of the authorities in Arab Jerusalem, their creation of faits accomplis and the serious demographic changes they had forced.

Avi-Shaul testified as deputy chairperson of the League of Human and Civil Rights. He was widely interviews and photographe A sick man, in his 80s, he had come all the way from Tel Aviv to tell the truth about injustice.

Nikara raised the legal aspects of the oppression and spoke of the occupier's laws. Many committee members and journalists heard for the first time of the Emergency Regulations Acts of 1945,

inherited from the British, labelled as fascist at the time by Jewish
lawyers, among them one who later became Minister of Legal
Affairs, S Shapira. "These regulations are now used to oppress
in the occupied territories and military commands and hundreds
of orders have been made and added."

When my turn came I told of the suffering I see every day.
I submitted my book, With My Own Eyes, as a document, and state
that on the basis of what I know of international law, and what I
have myself seen, the Israeli occupation authorities are guilty of
war crimes in the occupied territories.

Suliman sits in the row behind me, denied his homeland.
But he is alive, for Laila and his children, and his people whom he
loves so much.

We remember together the days of detention. "I was so
grateful to you on one occasion. When I was taken to Ramallah
at your request to see you. When the blindfold had been removed,
I could see the city through the window, the clear sky, the streets.
I love them so much, Felicia !"

One of the testimonies which shocked everyone was that
of a witness who could not come, under doctor's orders. This
was recorded by Ziad al-Ana of Bethlehem, whom I had not met.
Ziad was still in hospital in Moscow after the 'treatment' he
had received in Hebron. I will return to him later.

The work of the Council ended on 21 May. After hearing
testimonies from three representatives from Israel and three
expelled from the West Bank, and studying documents, recordings
and medical reports, a detailed summary was drawn up confirming
the existence of violations of human rights by Israelis in the occupied territories. It pointed out that the responsibility for acts of
oppression and mass terror rested with Israel's rulers, and
asked for all those carrying responsibility to be brought to trial.

In the press conference held after the hearings, the
Israeli Consulate circulated a petition saying, among other things,
that all in the West Bank was fine and that thousands of summer
visitors who came to see relatives could testify to it.

In a public appeal, the Council called on the world (a)
to condemn the outright violation of human rights in the occupied
Arab territories, (b) to put pressure on the Israeli Government
to free all political prisoners in the territories, end the torture,
stop the expulsions of residents and make it possible for those
already expelled to return home; (c) support the struggle of the
people in the occupied territories against the Israeli occupation;
(d) to honour international aggreements concerning human rights
in the territories and carry them out.

All criminal actions of the Israeli rulers of the area:
the mass arrests, tortures, murders, expulsions, annexations
of land, violation of UN decisions, all affect human society as a
whole, morally, politically and legally.

The forces of peace cannot sit idle while crimes are
committed in the territories by the Israeli authorities. Thus the
Council decided to turn over all its documents to the UN Council
on Human Rights, and to continue its activities so long as the
Israeli authorities continued with criminal actions   and Israeli
forces failed to leave the occupied territories.

The Israeli press was almost completely silent on the
events in Helsinki. We returned, strengthened, to continue the fight
for human rights.

MOTHER OF THE SHEIKH

"I have brought you almonds from our tree." She produces a full
sack, smiling. "Eat this bread, I baked it this morning at home.
The Sheikh can't eat it. May God watch over your children !"
I look at her, silently. She resembles the Sheikh, her 27-year-

old son, with his imposing appearance and burning eyes.

His present home is Kfar Yona prison, one of thousands of prisoners of the occupation. With him in the cell is his father, old and ailing, in jail for refusing to help with the arrest of his son.

Thus the mother has become responsible for the family. She sits opposite me and asks to hear about her son, devouring every word. She calls him 'Sheikh' with a pride that dries her tears and eases her tormented face. "The Sheikh has a new daughter. I'll bring her, and you'll see how beautiful she is, just like the Sheikh," she says, sighing again at the thought of him. "You see my grey hairs ? Do you understand ? I'll give you anything – take whatever you want....I want the Sheikh."

He has been sentenced to sixteen years. It was said that he would be made an example since he had reputedly joined Fatah as Imam (prayer leader) and had afterwards violated the commandments and the faith.

I appealed in order to put the Israeli 'military experts' on Islam in their place.

I read parts of the Koran, helped by Salah, and stated in the appeal that they presumed to peach morality to the accused in the name of Islam. I showed that Islam recognises the struggle for the homeland as a good deed.

The court of appeal reduced the sentence to thirteen years.

While he was in jail we became good friends. He was broadminded and clear thinking, and held a hunger strike with other administrative prisoners in the prison.

The Sheikh's mother brought his daughter to me: the beautiful baby, the grandmother's joy. Her other son was arrested and freed. She suffered all smiling, always encouraging the other women she met at my office.

Brave, dear mother of the Sheikh.

THE SECOND HUNGER STRIKE

In June 1975, after the detentions were extended, the prisoners started a hunger strike in protest. This was the second time, the first had been in February 1975.

Public circles in Nablus sent a letter to the military governor of the West Bank, protesting at the continued detention of West Bank residents.

The letter called for decisions on the prisoners to be hastened, and they should be freed or tried, since they had been detained a year and three months, contrary to international law.

It was sent to the Mayor of Nablus, and signed by women's organizations, representatives of industrial officers, the workers' union, union of doctors, lawyers and pharmacists and engineers, the Federation of Sports Club and the 'Hatain' Club.

It also declared that the prisoners unjustly detained were holding a hunger strike in protest, which endangered their lives, and that the detentions were in breach of the Geneva Convention, which Israel together with 52 other nations had signed in 1949.

The signatories stressed that the Convention determined "the detention of an administrative prisoner shall not continue longer than one month". They demanded the release of the detainees on the grounds of human dignity, right, justice and peace.

In Nablus, the hunger strike went on for eighteen days, and the danger to the prisoners was real. I was abroad, and Walid Fahum was in charge. He was prevented from seeing the prisoners. After my return from the USSR as one of a delegation of Israeli lawyers, I realised how stubborn the prisoners were, and how much support they had from public opinion in Israel and the occupied territories. The League of Human and Civil Rights held a vigil in front of the Prime Minister's office.

Communist Knesset members urgently requested that the prisoners' hunger strike be placed on the daily agenda.

"The prisoners are public figures, businessmen, workers, doctors, engineers - being held because of their political stand against the occupation and in favour of a just peace for their

people. The continuation of their imprisonment is in violation of
basic human rights."

MP Tawfiq Toubi raised the hunger strike in the Knesset
on 29 July, as it entered its third week.. He said the government
could not close its ears to the public demands to free the prisoners
without delay, after fifteen months of detention when there were
no charges for a trial.

He protested at the refusal to recognize the urgency of
the Communist Party's appeal concerning the continuing strike, now a
real danger to the prisoners' health.

An appeal from public figures to the Minister of Defence,
Shimon Peres, also published in the paper Ha-Aretz , declared:
"We are concerned for the hunger strike of administrative prison-
ers in the Nablus and Ramallah prisons. We join together to call
that they be brought to court or freed." This was signed by Uri
Avneri, Y Algazi, K Altman, Yibi, N Yalin Mor, Professor Dan
Meron, Professor A A Simon and Professor D Amit.

The sit-in strike of wives and relatives, on 29 July
at the Muslim Council in the Old City of Jerusalem, aroused great
interest. More than a hundred relatives signed a petition demanding that the prisoners be freed.

A delegation from the Movement of Democratic Women
in Israel made up of members from Tel Aviv and Jerusalem visited the
striking relatives and expressed support. Tawfiq Toubi and T
Ziad did likewise.

Toubi spoke to them, condemning the continuation of detention and violation of human rights, speaking of the strike as
part of the struggle against occupation.

Communist Knesset members raised the question with
other party members, sending an appeal to all members to support
the freeing of the prisoners.

The head of the Muslim Council visited the families and
announced support. Sheikh Halmi al-Muhtasib promised to sum-
mon the Council to discuss its response.

The strike ended after 23 days, but the struggle to free

the prisoners continued as many circles in Israel and throughout
the world protested at the detention.

MUHAMMAD YASIN

As I have said, I was determined to do everything possible to
annul Muhammad Yasin's trial. I was not satisfied with a normal
pardon – that is, a reduction of his eight year sentence by two or
three years – because that was the most to be expected. I aimed
at something much better, which would help us in the future. The
judgement passed, thanks to violations of the law and the silencing
of the accused, was praised in the press, as was Colonel Orion,
for his legal 'innovations'.

On meeting the police legal adviser in 'Judea and Samaria'
(the West Bank) I told him I would appeal to the High Court of Appeal.
Even if I failed, as I had in the past, at least I could show the
judges how the military courts enact their own laws.

My request was answered. The regional commander
cancelled the trial and set a retrial for September 1975. It was
covered by the press, and Zu Ha-Derech wrote on 17 September:

"On 8-9 September Muhammad Yasin's retrial was held before
a different set of judges headed by Colonel Feld. The new prosecutor from Nablus, Colonel M Zahavi, was military prosecutor.

"As permitted in a preliminary hearing, allowed on this occasion,
(it must be remembered that it had been forbidden in Yasin's
first trial) Yasin gave an account of his torture by the Shin Beit
during investigation He described how cold water was thrown
on him, how he was beaten on his head, ears, and entire body
while naked, and how cigarettes were extinguished on his body.

He showed the court a scar still visible on his face."

The testimony of the Shin Beit was a combination of arrogance and pretended innocence as they described the 'ideal' standards which they claimed prevailed during Yasin's investigation.

I stopped them and explained that one of them, Abu Nabil, (Yasin claimed to have seen him beat others many times, though he had never been beaten by him) had been with me at the time in Yagur prison. He had seen, as I had, the wounds on the bodies of Suliman al-Najab and Halil Hajazi. Despite this, he had declared before the Supreme Court, where complaints of prisoners about torture were heard, "that though I was present with Attorney Langer at the visit, I saw nothing..." "There is no value, in my eyes, in the testimony of such a man," I emphasized.

The judge intervened, "But you don't claim that this man beat Yasin, so why the attack against him ?" I replied that Abu Nabil covered up the torture, which was a crime in itself.

At the end of the preliminary hearing Yasin's statement was accepted, after the court determined that it believed "without hesitation" the testimony of the Shin Beit...

"I am opposed to occupation with all my heart, but my way was to fight it politically. I do not hate Jews. I feel brotherhood with all workers everywhere. I was educated in the fraternity of nations and I believe in peace between our peoples, without occupation or oppression. I did not go to the USSR to train in arms, but to learn," concluded Yasin.

After a short consultation, Yasin was found guilty on all counts: of belonging to the National Palestinian Front, of training in arms in the Soviet Union, and of enlisting friends to the Front.

Clearly the prosecution intended to confirm the eight - year sentence given at the first trial. For this purpose, they brought a Shin Beit 'expert' in Communism into the box to 'open the eyes' of the court to the 'dangers of the Front and the essence of Communism'. I objected to the witness, calling it a plot against the accused. A dispute broke out.

In the end the Shin Beit 'expert' did not give evidence, and was brought down from the witness box.

The prosecutor demanded an eight year sentence, quoting harsh sentences from the past in justification, even though for quite different offences.

In my turn I quoted sentences for similar offences, and requested that his sentence should not be disproportionate. I pointed out that the first sentence had been cancelled by the district commander, and if the result was now the same, the cancellation would appear merely as show.

Yasin was given three years and a three year suspended sentence.

GAZA PRISON

Few know about Gaza prison for women, though the men's prison is well known for its harsh conditions.

Testimony about it was given to Salah Badina and myself by an Arab woman prisoner from Ramallah, Ramia Uda, now serving in Neve Tirzah prison. She was taken there again from Gaza after serving there two months as punishment for attempting to escape from Neve Tirzah.

"The cells are 1 metre by 1.8 metres, with no window looking outside. In the corner is an open lavatory. A bright electric light shines day and night. The small window of my cell looked into the investigation room, and I heard the screams of those being beaten. It was extremely hot and humid in the cell. Those inside are not let out for the usual outing (an hour a day). I was let

out because of my poor health. Prisoners sit for two, sometimes three, months in these cells during investigation, to
break them. It is effective, because one can go out of one's
mind from the suffocating heat and stench, when one eats and
uses the lavatory in the same room. I couldn't eat at all.
There are no regular mattresses. I slept on an air mattress
less than a centimetre thick..

"In the general cell are the women who have finished investigation. There are no regular mattresses there either. For
an hour a day there is a 'trip' outside. The rest of the time
is spent in sitting on the floor on the air mattresses. During
the day you are allowed to sit, not to lie down. It is forbidden
to talk of politics or raise your voice. Even a normal conversation which creates any echo at all is punished severely, as
they claim it disturbs the warders. One of the most severe
punishments is to stop you going to the lavatory. Those being
punished are forced to use a pail in their rooms, which
greatly disturbs the dozens of women in the room.

"They allow only one shower a week, and the intense heat
in the cells in summer is an added torture.

"Medical treatment is a sort of gloating over the misfort-
unes of others. A diagnosis is given to stop the demands and
prevent an appeal to the Red Cross. The doctors, if and when
they come, list the treatment and medication as a mere form-
ality. Their instructions are never carried out, as they claim
there is no equipment or medicine, and no hope of treating
the patients as needed.

"Meetings with the Red Cross are an experience in themselves. The complainant risks her life. Revenge is not slow
in coming. Anything she wants, she is answered with "ask
the Red Cross. We don't have anything. If you have such a
big mouth, get it yourself. You won't get anything from us."
Of course this has its effect on those who appeal, fearing that
their condition will get even worse after their complaint.

"An additional torture comes during the women's menstrual

cycle, when she is not given enough sanitary towels, and
sometimes she is literally covered in blood. On the sign
'Gaza Prison' should be written 'Gaza Hell'."

About five months later I saw the cells in Gaza prison,
but I was forbidden to publish what I had seen.

ZIAD AL-GAZA AGAINST THE STATE OF ISRAEL

An Israeli court was to try a judicial case. The date is still not
known. The subject is damage caused by the agents of the state
of Israel to the plaintiff, Ziad al-Gaza, now twenty years old, a
refugee from the Bethlehem area. As I have previewed what is
to come, let us return to the description of the accused, Ziad
al-Gaza.

I became acquainted with him for the first time in May
1975 in Helsinki during the investigations of the committee on
the violation of human rights in the Arab occupied territories
since 1967 for the World Council for Peace.

His testimony was recorded, as I mentioned before.
Silence reigned in the hall, and from the loudspeaker came his
hoarse voice and broken sentences. He described how he had
been arrested without being charged; and his torture in Hebron
prison, as a result of which he was still in hospital in the
Soviet Union. The testimony was difficult to follow, and
at the end a short medical statement was read, from which
we understood that he had suffered brain damage. Because
of this, the normal functioning of his body was severely
impaired.

I suddenly felt very close to the young boy I had never

seen, whose trembling voice aroused emotion in the committee,
whose members came from many nations and had many viewpoints.
I remembered the days in May 1974 when his family had appointed
me his lawyer, and how I was prevented from seeing him for a
long time.

One day I received information that he was being tortured
and that I must do everything possible to see him. I went to
Hebron, and in the prison hall I met the prosecutor, Colonel Moshe
Farkash. I insisted he take me to meet Ziad and told him of my
fears for him, and that I would appeal to the High Court of Appeals
if he would not agree. Then came the answer, whose meaning I
did not then fully understand. Farkash said very pleasantly that
there was no truth in the rumour and that he was in excellent shape.
Why should I make trouble over nothing when he, Farkash, declared
before me (but in secret) that Ziad was to be freed the following
week. Why interview him in jail when he was already half out ?

It was clear that even if I appealed to the High Court it
would be more than a week before I could see him, so I decided to
wait and test Farkash's declaration. I must admit I did not con-
sider the possibility that Ziad's condition was making Farkash do
everything to stop me seeing him. After seven days he was freed
and sent straight to the hospital for nervous disorders in Bethlehem.
His bad condition served as the reason for his release. I did not
get to see him there. I was then told that he had got worse and had
been sent by his family to the Soviet Union for treatment.

In a Moscow apartment belonging to friends I met Ziad.
He looked extremely young, and had tears in his eyes. He had just
been discharged from hospital. He squeezed my hand and smiled.
He gripped the edge of the table to stop his hand shaking. His right
leg shook like a leaf. He was pale and I grasped his arm firmly.
"I wanted very much to see you in jail. Once, friends of the prison-
ers told me that you had come and I was so happy. But afterwards
I understood that you hadn't been allowed to see me."

He asked about his friends still rotting in prison. He told
me that the hand he had given me had no feeling, that the Soviet

doctors had performed a miracle. "I don't hate those who did this to me at all. Please give my greetings to all who want peace and who understand that my people must be given their rights." Suddenly he began to talk about 'there', about the cells, the torture. We are absorbed in our thoughts, and around us our friends understand our silence. "We'll meet again tomorrow," we said.

He sits facing me and begins to talk about what happened to him in prison. He has long wanted to tell me, but now when the time has come he doesn't know where to begin. I ask when he was arrested.

It was on 23 April 1974. Israeli soldiers came to our house in the al-Gaza refugee camp near Bethlehem. When they had surrounded and searched the house, they arrested me. At first they asked me, "Here are Israeli soldiers, aren't you scared ?" "Why should I be ? You're only flesh and blood," I answered.

They took me to Hebron prison and the investigation began. One of the investigators said to me "You are a member of the Jordanian Communist Party. You distributed their pamphlets in Bethlehem University. It's useless to deny it. Jacky the investigator is very quick. He investigated the Syrian prisoners. There are a lot of us, and we change places among the eight of us when we get tired. They pay us well. It would even be worth it for you to work with us. We get 100 pounds for an investigation like this. You ought to know we can extract secrets, even from the ground. We have dogs, we have electricity. Why should you take all this ? You'd go out of here crazy and even your friends would throw you to the dogs. What use is a crazy person to them ?" Suddenly one broke in, "Give us fifteen minutes. You don't need all the other things. He'll start talking by himself." "Is this your democracy ?" I asked.

Then Jacky came up to me and boxed my ears with all his might. They tied my hands behind and took me to the cell.

I asked him if this cell was on the second floor and he said yes. I remembered these cells. I had seen them by court order. The rough walls, concrete floors with thin air mattresses, a space only big enough to spread out in, and a pail as a lavatory. No air, no light.

He continued:

They brought me a few olives and potatoes and put them on the floor as if I were a dog. The guard kicked the food. I didn't eat it, and after a few minutes they took me down to the investigating room.

They began with threats that they would bring my whole family here if I didn't tell them the truth about Husni Hadad and the others from Bethlehem. I told them they had taken our land from us, made us refugees with nothing, and now asked me to imprison innocent people - and if not, they would arrest my family. "Bring them, all of them. Their lives are not lives anyway. But you won't make me into such a despicable creature." Then Jacky began to scream, "Son of a bitch, you don't even care for the fate of your family and what we'd do to your mother and father. Never mind. Now they'll take you to a place where you'll talk. They'll give you a shot. It will affect your mind and make you into a woman afterwards, but you'll talk for sure."

Then they tied my hands behind me and stripped me naked, since I refused to strip myself. I was beaten all over, and fainted. When I came round, they had put something that burned like fire on my sexual organs. All this time I was blindfolded. They removed the blindfold and again ordered me to talk. I told them nothing would help them, that the wheels of history could not be put back, and that the day would come when they would have to account for everything. "You whore" they shouted, and brought a syringe. They told me I would become a girl unless I told them the names of my colleagues. I told them I did not have any, that I was one of the people, and that if they wanted, I would give them the names of everyone in Gaza refugee camp.

Suddenly he stopped speaking, grew very pale, and held
on to the edge of the table. "Don't worry, it will pass." After
a few minutes he continued,

Then they brought someone whom they introduced as a psychia-
trist from the University. He spoke fluent Arabic, and brought in
an Arabic saying to persuade me to talk: that if I did not talk
like Musa, I would talk like Pharaoh (if not in good, then in
evil). 'When we were children,' he said, 'we read adventure
stories while you learned about Julius Volshik and Georgy Dim-
itrov. They are all a lot of nonsense.' He turned to Jacky,
'This son of a bitch is talking philosophy to me.' Jacky kicked
me angrily, saying, 'You dog, this is a doctor, not a tramp
from the streets like you.' 'Now you can see the nice treatment for yourself, doctor,' I said.

I was taken to the cell, and thought that was the end for the
day, but I was brought back after a short time, and they said,
'We have given you time to think about your ideas. Until now,
we have just been playing games. From now on we are serious.'
They hung me up by the legs - you can still see the black mark
on my ankle. Then they beat my head and pulled my hair. I
was naked, and I thought I'd go out of my mind. When they took
me down, blood poured from my eyes. 'They laughed, saying,,
'Now we'll see Captain Johnny come !'

He came and I spat at him. He just wiped it from his face
and said, 'Now you're going to be a girl.' He put something
up my anus from a bottle. It hurt a lot and I was beside myself.
He asked if I liked it, and said it would continue every day.
I ached all over and my head was burning. This last humiliation
was almost too much.

In my heart I decided it would be better to die, but first I
wanted revenge for all they had done. I suddenly announced
that I was ready to talk as they wished, but that first they
must untie me and give me a cup of coffee. This made them
happy, and they did what I asked.

I knew they prepared coffee near a glass cabinet. The moment
Jacky's back was turned as he leaned over it, I went and
smashed him into it. I hoped that the broken glass would leave
scars on their faces for the rest of their lives. If I died at
their hands, so much the better. But the glass cut my right
hand - here is the scar - and hardly touched them.

They jumped and screamed at me, and took me back to the
cell at once with my hand bleeding and senses blurred. Then
began the second period, when I received salty food and no
water. That was in Basa prison in Bethlehem. As you see,
they broke my nose.

Then I came back to Hebron. In the investigating room,
something was put on my head, like earphones, and I felt an
electric shock go through me. Horrible convulsions shook me,
and I felt as if I was going to burst. They screamed over and
over again 'Talk !' and I answered 'Dogs !' Again the shock
passed through me, look, here, near my fingernails they operated on me. My nails fell out or were badly damaged, as they
still are. My body is covered in cigarette burns from their
revenge. After the shocks I was again beaten till my right arm
and leg felt paralysed. They had to carry me, for I couldn't
walk.

And then, apparently afraid that I really would die, they
freed me. They took me to hospital in Bethlehem, and from
there to Moscow. I'll never forget the Soviet doctors. One
of them cried when she saw me. At one time I was almost
blind, and afraid I was always going to be like that. I was in
hospital for nine months, undergoing all manner of treatment
to become as you see me now. The doctors joked that I had
a pharmacy in my stomach.

Felicia, send my greetings to all those who protest at injustice. I was strong because I felt them with me.

We part, embracing as friends. He is moved and his hand
again begins to shake. He looks older than he is, and there is

something tragic in the childlike smile.

THE 'TESTIMONY'

The open space before the military court in Gaza is deserted. It is 9 January 1975. A raging wind sets flying the veils of the women waiting for their husbands and sons to come from the nearby prison. They arrive in a military truck, and the women rush to see them close up. The soldiers act, ordered by the guard, Eliahu Atias, known for his zeal. 'Remove them immediately, 'he yells, and the women are pushed off.

I ask to speak to my client, Hasan Abiad, among the prisoners. Atias decides 'no', and his face expresses satisfaction with this demonstration of authority. But his 'no' is ignored as I approach the truck and speak to Hasan. Atias turns to the military guards, 'Do something !' But they are too late, and we finish our conversation.

My assistant, Haim, is confused by the guards' vulgarity however Atias points to the tape recorder he is carrying, "You won't go into court with that! " Haim says he will ask the judge's permission and there the matter ends, or appears to.

The prisoners go into the cell to await the trial. There are nine of them, Hasan Abiad, Muhammad Jarda, Ahmad Rian, Jamil al-Rifi, Hasan Hamuda, Hasan Jakari, Jamil Odallah, Ali Sheikh, and Ahmad Shaban. Hasan Hamuda is eighty-three years old. He is not here by mistake; the indictment says he was born in 1892. He has no teeth, but he says, "I did have a few, but they beat me and they fell out. I'm accused of possessing guns which I know nothing about." The group as a whole is accused of bel-

longing to Fatah, of possessing arms, and of carrying out various
acts.

Hasan Abiad looks ill. His face is yellow, and he has lost
eleven kilos during his detention. He complains that he was badly
beaten by the Shin Beit at his investigation at the police station.

The trial begins. Advocates Akila and Abu Warda present
their cases. One of the judges puts his gun on the table. Near it
is a knitted skull cap, which someone apparently left there. The
skull cap, the revolver, the state flag and the Arab accused.

Eliahu Atias rises, and testifies that he found a plastic
bag containing bullets in Hasan's house. He states that Hasan
was warned that he did not have to talk, but that if he did his
words would be used in evidence against him in court. I question
him about his knowledge of Arabic, and it is clear that he does
not know how to express the warning in Arabic. He gets confused
and tangled in lies throughout the examination. Abu Warda gives
him a short test in simple Arabic and Eliahu is helpless. He is
no longer arrogant.

Two prisoners plead guilty. The prosecutor states that
he has been instructed to give severe punishments in a time like
the present, of rising activity against the occupation. The 'light'
sentences of the past have not been effective.

The trial of the rest of the prisoners is then postponed.

THE HOUSE

Before the trial I visited Shati refugee camp on the beach with
members of Hasan's family. His sister showed me the remains
of their house, destroyed by order of the military governor.

It had been small, but had provided shelter for six people. The family had been given half an hour to remove their belongings, and had not managed to take everything. What remained was buried under the ruins. It was Haim's first visit to a refugee camp. He looked at the ruins, and said, "The way they live here, and even what they have is destroyed."

IBRAHIM

"This is Ibrahim's wife," says his mother.

"Was he arrested at night ?" I asked her. "Yes. The soldiers came at three o'clock in the morning." "Did they come into the bedroom ?" "Yes, we have only one room which is both living and bed room. They ordered us to dress, and even searched the bed. Then they took him away."

His mother spoke, "My son is twenty-two. You know how I brought him up ? I worked as a servant carrying wood and water, doing other people's washing, for his sake and his brother's. We have lived as refugees in the Kalandia camp since 1948. Do you know Beit Shemesh ? We owned three large plots of land there, twenty dunums of olive trees and vineyards. What would you have done in our place ? They fired on our village and we had no arms to defend ourselves. We gathered all we could and fled."

Ibrahim was sentenced to twelve years in prison.

YOUTH BEHIND BARS

Nablus prison is full of high school and college students fervently protesting against the occupation. "When it started we were about ten or twelve years old. Eight years have toughened us. We were moved from the large prison to this small one," said Loai Jayusi. He is eighteen, a high-school student. But his handsome face looks much older. He and his friends were taken from school to jail, accused of being members of Fatah and of recruiting for it.

At his house we met his grandmother, grandfather, sisters, brothers and parents. His father began. "We will never forget that night. Soldiers came with their fingers on the triggers of their guns..."

By beatings, the authorities forced Loai and his friends (Muhammad al-Usta, Ikram Sharif, Muhammad al-Hanafi, Naif Abu Alyan and Mustafa al-Hagsh) to confess that every member of the Jordanian Communist Party was automatically a member of the Palestinian National Front. Membership of the PNF was illegal, and a member could be sentenced to up to ten years in prison. One of the boys said, "We wrote anti-occupation slogans on the walls. We confessed this during our investigation..."

The youngsters were taken back to their cells and I left the prison. On my way back I saw hundreds of students in the streets going home at the end of the school day, young people without rights, without any possibility of national expression. I wondered how many of them I would meet behind bars.

RAMLE PRISON

Muhammad Madi Besisu, a young Palestinian from Gaza, was serving his sentence in the central prison at Ramle. He was sent to the prison hospital with a head wound and a broken arm.

He had been arrested on 24 May 1971 on board a boat, beyond the limits of Israel's territorial waters. He assumed he would not be tried because the Israeli courts had no jurisdiction. But, after he had spent two years in detention, Israel amended its penal code to make it effective anywhere in the world where the security of Israel was involved. On 26 February 1973 the District Court of Beersheva sentenced him to fifteen years for association with Fatah and similar charges.

After the trial he was returned to prison. There the authorities accused him of inciting fellow prisoners to declare a hunger strike. He was transferred to Ramle and was held in solitary confinement for fourteen months. Then he was transferred again to Askelon. There too he was accused of making trouble and inciting prisoners. Muhammad denied this new charge, saying that "if a guard tries to humiliate a prisoner, the prisoner knows how to defend himself."

He was taken back to Ramle where he was again held in solitary confinement, for three months, twenty-three hours a day. He was denied concessions given to other prisoners, such as a shower twice a week and reading material. When a sergeant once denied him a shower, he asked for better treatment. The sergeant got angry and hit him with a bunch of keys, cursing his family. Muhammad could not endure this and hit back with a spoon, cursing in his turn.

Within fifteen minutes, about twenty guards, with officers, came to his cell with clubs. They dragged him out into the corridor and beat him till he fell bleeding, unable to move. Lt Gazlan kicked his stomach several times, causing him anguish because of his ulcer. They then dragged him back to the cell. The prison director arrived and expressed amazement at

what had happened. "The jailors are strong - why did they use
clubs ?" But everything was excused on the grounds that Muhammad had struck the sergeant. A doctor came and gave him first aid.
He spent the night in the dirty cell, and only in the morning was
his head shaved and the wounds dressed. He was not given anti-
biotics, and only when the gravity of his condition had become obvious was he taken to a nearby hospital. There, X-rays showed
that his arm was broken in several places. It was put in a cast
and he was returned to solitary confinement. A few days later
he was worse, and was moved to the prison hospital.

I asked the Red Cross to intervene and they took care of
the matter. Meanwhile attorney Ghazi Kuffair saw Muhammad.
I visited him on 8 October 1975 and got a statement from him,
and saw the remains of his wounds. The cast had been recently
removed and his arm was still paralysed. I submitted a complaint
to the Minister of Police, but it was rejected on the grounds that
Muhammad was to blame for what had happened.

THE HIGH PRICE

On Tuesday morning 16 September 1975 people in the military
court at Nablus saw an unusual sight. In the dock was a very old and
sick man. He had been arrested some time ago. His sons had
been previously arrested, and all but one had been released. This
son, Loai, was accused of bringing explosives to Israel's international airport. He had been badly beaten in the presence of his
father in an effort to get a confession from him. The old man's
name was Ali Nafi Abdu, and the court was sitting to decide whether
to release him on bail.

Suddenly he went into convulsions, lay down, and screamed. We called for emergency aid, but no-one moved. One of the officers remarked, "He was put up to this."

I went to the judge's room and explained the situation to him, asking for him to be released on bail, since he could not escape. "I am not a doctor, and know nothing of medicine," he replied.

"But the judges of the High Court of Justice aren't doctors either, and they released Yoshua Ben-Zion on bail after he had been convicted of stealing forty-seven thousand dollars. They based their ruling on medical testimony. You only have to follow the High Court ruling, Your Honour." But he ignored my plea and gave no answer.

Meanwhile, the court turned to another case. I stayed with the old man till his doctor, Dr Hatim Abu Gazala of Nablus, arrived. When he saw the old man lying on the dirty floor, he said, "I will not treat him while he is left like this." But no-one answered.

"Don't you agree that the Shin Beit are in control here ?" I asked him. One of the Shin Beit men smiled, saying, "To prove that we treat people humanely we'll bring a bed for him at once." A few minutes later a bed was brought and the man placed on it.

"This man is seriously ill. He does not know where he is, his words are incoherent. His blood pressure is high, he has diabetes and one of his kidneys is inflamed. I recommend his immediate transference to hospital" said the doctor in his report.

The judge said, "Take him away, I have no objection to that.

But the prosecutor said, "He must not be moved. The prison doctor will come and report on his actual condition."

In the meantime the prison doctor and his assistant arrived. They injected him with something and he fell asleep. The doctor, a lieutenant in the army, testified, and was examined by Walid Fahum. He said the patient's life was not in danger, and that he should be returned to prison, where he would be treated. The request for bail was rejected, and the man returned to prison, still asleep.

Everyone in the court saw the indifference of the soldiers and police.

JAIL IS GOOD FOR HIM

The military court in Lod was unusually crowded on 10 November. The dock was hardly big enough for all the young Arabs in it. Two were charged with an unusual crime, membership of the Syrian Baath Party, and, for the other, membership of the Iraqi Baath Party. Another was a fifteen-year-old accused with membership of an illegal 'union'.

After the reading of the indictments, all charges were denied, except those attributed to a boy who appeared utterly indifferent to what was going on. When the others left the dock, their trials postponed, he remained. His name was Ibrahim Kamouk, from East Jerusalem, and he was accused of associating with an illegal organization and attempting to make explosives.

He had gone insane during detention. I had heard this through other families visiting relatives in prison. The parents had not been officially notified.

The father and I had received permission to see the boy together. He did not recognize his father, and retreated when the father tried to go to him. On his neck and hands were burns from cigarettes.

The medical assistant claimed they were self-inflicted, but no-one knew how, as he had been in solitary confinement. His father said he did not smoke. I asked how they could give him cigarettes in his present state, and also why they had not treated his wounds before they became infected. "As you see, he seems to feel no pain," answered the medic.

I demanded his immediate transfer to a mental hospital; because his continued stay in prison could lead to his death or irrevocable insanity. Suddenly the boy began to hit his head against the wall, the father trying to stop him. Attempts to talk to him were vain. Ibrahim lay down on the floor and refused to get up. Two jailors came and dragged him screaming to the cell. We left the prison.

The prison director cabled us authority to transfer him to the psychiatric ward at Ramle immediately. I was assured that he was transferred the next morning.

Fahum outlined Ibrahim's situation to the court. When the judges realised he could not stand trial, they ordered his return to the hospital for intensive treatment until he was fit enough to be tried.

At the second session he showed some improvement. The judge said to me, "Isn't he better than the last time we saw him ? Jail was good for him."

At the end, the public attorney said that mental illness could be treated in prison. I objected. After long consultations both the majority and minority decisions were read out. The minority sentenced him to six years in prison, the majority to three. Ibrahim reacted with a blank smile.

THE BOOKS

A referendum conducted in the prisons of the occupied territories on the kinds of books the inmates most enjoy reading would show that they preferred Marx and political economy.

A prisoner by the name of Rami Livneh once filed an application to the High Court of Justice to allow prisoners to read Marxist books. He succeeded, but the authorities claimed that the ruling did not apply to the occupied territories. Thus a prisoner in Ramle, even one from the West Bank, could read such books, but if he was transferred to Askelon, it was no longer allowed.

I visited Ali al-Jafari and Ahmad Tallib in Askelon, and during the visited, in the presence of the prison director, they repeated their request. They said there were many books on political economy in the prison, and the director said the guards would remove them at once.

Both prisoners said, "We are political prisoners. Is it not enough to imprison our bodies? Must they also imprison our minds?"

After getting no satisfaction from the prison director, I decided to appeal again to the High Court of Justice.

RASHID

Rashid al-Shamrouk, born in the al-Dahisha refugee camp, was ten when the occupation began.

At seventeen, he and his friends joined an illegal organi - zation, and in January 1975 he was arrested and charged with ass- ociating with it, attempting to recruit others, and creating trouble (writing slogans on walls).

I was ill when the trial took place, and cabled the judge.
But he went on with the trial and sentenced Rashid to ten years.
He was not allowed to defend himself.

I protested and threatened to appeal to the High Court of
Justice on the grounds that the trial was in violation of the Geneva
Convention. The military commander agreed to annul the sentence,
and ordered a retrial before a different judge. But on each of the
three occasions set for the retrial, the prisoner was not brought
from Beesheva jail.

Rashid was sentenced to eleven months, with two years
suspended sentence and a fine of five hundred Israeli pounds.

NAIM

His name is Naim Oda. He was sitting near a table in the reception
room at Hebron, brought to me from 'above' - in prison jargon, from
the solitary cells under direct control of the Shin Beit: they decide
which cell, number of blankets, showers, changes of clothes, if the
window is to be opened and the length of stay.

He said he had been there for twenty-two days without
seeing an investigator or being allowed to leave his cell. For
fourteen days before that he had been beaten all over while tied
by his hands to a bar of the window.

"Why were you so long in coming to see me this time ?
You used to come quickly," he said.

"Yes, Naim. I still remember those times I came to
visit you in prison. That time early in 1968, when Hebron was
covered in snow, and there was no water or electricity. Then

they brought you here in 1973, and now again, for the third time.
When I see you in those torn and dirty clothes, I ask myself,
the source of your courage."

'MABROUK'

It was 10 December, the day the Democratic Front won the
municipal elections in Nazareth and made Tawfiq Ziad Mayor.
As usual the guards at Nablus prison received me with hostility,
obstructing myself and my trainee Salah Badarna on the pretext
"We don't know him."

The prisoners began to arrive, young and old, of different organizations and ideologies. All seemed happy, repeating
'mabrouk' (congratulations), and full of hope.

"Give our greetings to Tawfiq. Nablus is not far from
Nazareth."

I did not leave till I had shaken hands with every prisoner,
as if we were all at a big party celebrating peace and friendship.

I left the prison gate with 'mabrouk' still ringing in my
ears, and it continued to do so for a long time. Full of courage,
it was the watchword in the battle to victory, victory of the dignity
of a great people.

SILENCE IS GOLDEN

Today's case is unusual. In the wounded city of Gaza everything is unusual.

We were at the court waiting to begin, but my mind was busy with another case, that of Fuad Makawi, a teacher in the UNRWA school at Khan Yunis. He was a graduate from the Teachers' Training College in Ramallah, married two months before his arrest. His wife later gave birth to a boy, whom they named after his father's code-name in the organization, al-Hammam. This practice became a tradition in the Gaza Strip after the June War.

There were nine defendants in the dock. Among them were Ismail Habib, Salih Amsha, Tawfiq al-Zara, Ramadan Batriha, Muhammad Habib. They were accused of attempting to steal arms from an Israeli soldier after offering him a ride in their car, and of plotting an illegal operation. They were acquitted of the attempted robbery but charged with the plotting, and thus given light sentences.

Before the trial a soldier asked me, "Suppose the soldier they trapped had been your son, what would you do?" I thought of my son Michael and replied, "My son preferred to go to jail rather than serve in the occupied territories."

The soldier said, "But they aren't occupied territories, they are our lands." I saw traces of doubt on another soldier's face but he didn't dare deviate from the given line. "You have been brainwashed for a long time, but a time will come when you will realize that our place is not here. Then there will be neither terrorists nor victims. The real criminals are those who sent you here."

A group of lawyers, including Abu Dikka, Abu Warda and Ukiala, are with me. Collectively, we asked permission to see Gaza prison and the conditions there, to examine the statements made by Ismail, who had spent thirty days there.

The public attorney consented, to our agreeable surprise. But the military judge, Lt Col Ore, looked disapproving. But it

was too late, and the court approved the application for a visit at
1.30 pm that same day.

We arrived to find the Shin Beit ready to receive us.
There were whispers, consultations, delays, and we had to wait
a full hour for their decision: 'The Shin Beit disapproves of the
visit because the place is "off limits to". The judge's face was red
with embarrassment as the decision was overruled.

We returned to court, and Abu Dikka criticized the
decision, saying that it was dangerous for a court not to carry out
its own orders.

Then I spoke. "Their decision not to allow us to see the
secrets of the cells proves there is something to hide. We believe
the court must order its decision to be enforced at once, and
refer to trial those who showed contempt for that decision."

Abu Warda demanded that the Shin Beit agents next to
the public attorney be interrogated. But the public attorney
intervened, "I withdraw my approval of the visit and ask the
court to reject the request."

I immediately said, "It is obvious that you are hardly
independent, and that your conscience is easily bought."

Taking no decision, the judge adjourned the trial to
4 January 1976, claiming it was too late in the day to continue.
The judge then allowed the visit, on condition that the subsequent
session be closed, and that nothing about the proceedings or the
visit be published.

We went, and on return presented the conclusion of our
defence, taking about an hour. The session was then opened to
the public.

As I recall, I addressed the court, "No whitewash in the
world will ever erase the black spot engraved on our minds by
what we have seen today."

The interpreter looked at the judge and translated my
statement into Arabic. But it was not recorded as part of the
session. It was heard and published afterwards....

There is a place in Gaza where silence is golden.

WADIDA HAMDAN

You are still young, but the disease threatens your life. It attacked suddenly when you were eight. Where is your kind father, Abd al-Majid, who gave you love and compassion and who is now behind bars in Hebron? No charge was made against him.

He came handcuffed to your bedside, and saw you, but you could not see him, because you were already blind. When they took him from prison he was not told where he was going. He did not know of your illness, and did not expect to find you blind. Words froze in his mouth.

People looked at him as a handcuffed criminal. His heart was shattered. So was your mother's, the courageous mother who bore her pain in silence.

People love you, Wadida. In far away Helsinki I told your story to Suliman, and he could not hold back his tears. I took your head in my hands and stroked your hair. I felt your warmth.

And now, after twenty-one months of administrative detention, your father sits beside you. I hope they find a cure for your disease, to restore you full of life and vitality once more. I hope to hear you sing, dear Wadida.

LIFE IN THE TOMBS

From behind an iron door marked with black figures, and a small opening in the wall with an iron shutter looking onto a corridor, I heard your low voice saying "Come in and see."

The jailor opened the door. The cell was humid and

dark, and for a tomb it was quite spacious - 2 metres by 1.40.
It could hold several corpses. There is no window, opening or
crack, nothing to suggest that there is a world outside.

But you have the needs of a living being. They provide
you with a pail for a lavatory, and containers for food and water.
You are, as your jailors emphasize, very well. My concern for
you springs from my ignorance of your Arab nature.

Your eyes are red. Your bed is a piece of rubber mat,
less than a centimetre thick, spread on a cement floor. "When
it rains the walls are wet," you say. For God's sake don't repeat
that, or the guards will get angry with us. They may return you
to your cell and shut the door. And so you will return to your
dampness and darkness, and I to the outside world.

MUHAMMAD BIHAIS

His name is Muhammad Naji Bihais, an old friend. It was my
first trial in Hebron, and he was the first young man to be sentenced to 25 years for his association with an illegal organization
and possessing a pistol. But time would break down that unjust
sentence.

In prison he had been beaten about the head till his eyes
almost popped out. The sentence was intended as the final blow
that would break him for ever.

I saw him in Askelon and Beersheva prisons, but later
I was so busy with other cases that I got diverted from his.

In January 1976, several years later, I saw him in
Nablus prison. It was an emotional meeting and I was anxious
to hear what he had to say.

"I was arrested when quite young, and at the time was motivated by nationalist zeal. For many years now I have suffered the hardships of prison life. But over the years my ideas have matured. I have had a chance to read a lot, and one of the books was by Tawfiq Ziad. Please convey to him my congratulations on his becoming Mayor of Nazareth. He doesn't know me, but tell him I share his ideas." When he saw my admiration, he said, "Don't be amazed. People change. They have jailed my body, but how could they jail my mind ?"

IBRAHIM GARAIBA

He smiled at me with his wide and beautiful eyes, and began his story. "I was arrested last September at my father's house in Tlut, near Tulkarem. They found some leaflets against the occupation among my things. I wrote them alone, on my own initiative. Who can remain silent ? You also distribute leaflets, don't you ? I am twenty. I had finished high school and wanted to study law. Our people need lawyers. Let's go back to my arrest. They took me to Nablus and beat me. The two beating me were called Micha and James. They pulled out my hair and beat my testicles, and threatened to break my arms and give me artificial ones, like my legs." He paused to show me, "I have no legs. But I have a heart, a mind, dignity, and I love the soil of my homeland."

His voice was hoarse. He continued, "This is the stick I lean on. It's new - the interrogators broke the other one. They cursed me with every word they could think of. Solitary confinement was the hardest thing for me, but now I am with the other prisoners and they help me in every way."

The interview was over. One of Ibrahim's friends
helped him to stand, and he walked slowly, leaning on his stick.
I followed him with my eyes. He turned as if he felt them, and
smiled, and his eyes shone before he vanished beyond the iron
door. I imagined him with his artificial legs, with the interrogators standing erect before him. He could not move, nor feel
the soil of his homeland, but he loves it none the less.

IMPROPER WORDS

The day for the trial came. Dozens of prisoners including
Ibrahim sat in a narrow cell near the hall of the court. Accompanied by Abed Asali I entered the cell. Abed wanted to see for
himself what was happening. "I see a whole class of pupils,"
he said. One prisoner answered, "There are six who weren't
brought today." Ibrahim could not stand, and I asked for a chair
for him. The police answered, "Do you want him to break it
on our heads "?

"How could he, with artificial legs ?" I asked, "Are you
afraid of him ?"

"We won't give him a chair. He can sit on the floor,"
they answered. Ibrahim put aside his legs and sat on the cold
concrete. It was cold - the police were wearing overcoats.
"You see he's happy, sitting on the floor," one of them says.

I look for something for him to sit on, but found nothing
but my robe, which he refused. I insisted till he accepted it.
But it reached him only after a thorough inspection.

At 1 pm the judges arrived. The prisoners were accused
of association with the PFLP and Fatah, and of distributing anti-

Israel leaflets. Ibrahim was also accused of recruiting others.

They confessed to some of the charges. Before the verdict, Ibrahim testified under oath. He spoke of his miserable childhood. Born deformed, he could only crawl. In 1969 both legs were amputated at Bethlehem Hospital. At Tel Hashomer Hospital he had been given artificial legs. He struggled till he graduated from high school, and he wanted to study law. But his father abandoned him after marrying a second wife.

"Didn't they give you free treatment at Tel Hashomer ?" asked the judge.

"No. The Red Cross paid the bill."

"But did they treat you well ?"

"Yes."

"And yet you did all this."

"Are you referring to the distribution of leaflets ?" I interrupt.

"It is in his own interests. Stop interrupting," said the judge.

There was another prosecutor sitting next to the public attorney, who declared he was attending as an observer. When the public attorney referred to Ibrahim in his presentation of the case, this 'observer' whispered something to him which made him adopt a firmer attitude.

"You declared that you were only an observer," I broke in.

"He has the right to intervene as he wishes," replied the judge.

The public attorney said that Ibrahim was one of the leaders, and thus very dangerous. He also said that all but two of the other accused were also dangerous. He asked that the two be released, as they had already served two months. For Ibrahim he demanded a ten-year sentence.

Meanwhile, one of the defence lawyers made a strange request: that the court hear the testimony of one of the witnesses in closed session. The witness, he said, 'is a citizen of the same place". He also stipulated that I should not be present.

Of course I objected. I had never heard of such a request.
I explained that as the lawyer defending the other prisoners, I had
to hear all testimonies made to the court, adding "this is an unprecedented scandal."

"Your language is improper", remarked the judge.

The public attorney and police were pleased with the
judge's stand.

"And if we separate the case of the lawyer's client from
the others so that it would not be prejudicial to them, would you
then agree ?"

I knew I had no choice...

I opened my defence by discussing the question of 'work'
in Israel. I said that we seemed to give Arabs from the occupied
territories work as a charity and expect them to be grateful.
"The Geneva Convention provides that we should secure work for
them either where they live or in Israel. Undoubtedly we want
them to work to build up our state. If so, why the hypocrisy ?"

I continue my defence. Soon the day is over and darkness
falls. It seemed that the judges were too tired to be able to give
a verdict that day.

IBRAHIM GARAIBA

Again I was in Nablus with my trainee Abed Asali. Abed was born
in the village of Kari, and from a tender age he had known what it
was like to be an Arab in Israel. But he did not yet know what it
was to be one of a people without rights, like those of the occupied
territories.

It was 28 January, and Nablus was in a state of siege. Armoured vehicles were parading the streets and soldiers carried their weapons with a finger on the trigger. They were crowding the streets ready for any emergency, because of student demonstrations against the American veto at the UN Security Council.

There had been several demonstrations in schools that morning, and in some schools classes had been cancelled. The residents called it the 'renewed occupation'.

I remembered an Israeli Television programme I had seen months ago, after the demonstrations. An Israeli soldier stood by his car, his rifle held up with his finger on the trigger. In the background was a Nablus school. The narrator had said, "Classes have returned to normal in Nablus."

In a small cell-like room in the court, the prisoners waited. This time, unlike the last, Ibrahim was given a chair. I said to him, "This is a small victory."

Suddenly I was called to the judges' chamber, where I was told that a new judge would be deputizing, an act provided for in law. "How will he know what has happened in previous sessions ?" I asked.

The president said he would ask him to go through the minutes. When I saw the minutes, I found that only ten sentences of my defence had been included. I objected, and asked to be allowed to repeat my arguments to the new judge. This was accepted.

The judges arrived and the president read the verdict. He said that distributing leaflets and associating with a hostile organization would obstruct normal life in the occupied territories, and sentenced the accused to prison terms ranging from four to fourteen months, in addition to two years' suspended sentence. One of them, Mustafa, got fourteen months, a harsh sentence for the charge against him. At Ibrahim's turn, the president reminded the spectators that he was 'ungrateful', that he 'did what he did' even after getting treatment at Tel Hashomer Hospital in Israel. The president continued, "But the court has taken his condition into consideration." He was sentenced to six years, four of them suspended. "This is as far as we can go in condoning his actions. If you look for more, you must petition the military governor. Perhaps he will commute his sentence."

Ibrahim stood up, leaning on his friend's shoulder. I recalled his words, "If a people are determined to survive, nothing will stop them."

ABU OMAR

He was standing before me in the prison corridor, his face pale and his eyes hollow. I was used to seeing pale faces, but every time I was afraid. He told me the story of his almost unbearable torture, imposed in an attempt to break him. But they failed. His voice was tremulous, but his eyes still shone. That sparkle in his eyes was a symbol of his strength.

He had suffered much in his life. He had been persecuted for his ideas since he was fourteen. His people were thirsty for enlightenment. The king's interrogators had tried to subdue him by force, but the years he spent in prison turned him to steel.

He felt pain in every part of his body. He could not sleep. But he was always smiling, looking to the future he believed in. He loved his people and hated the occupation, and was ready to talk of his beliefs. But the interrogators wanted names and details of operations he knew nothing about. So, all efforts with him were vain. His wife sat at home and wrote poetry about her imprisoned husband.

CHILDREN IN COURT

She was eleven, but looked even younger. The policewomen
held her by her hands. Next to her is a boy of the same age, and
several others aged thirteen to sixteen. One of them, aged fifteen,
has his arm in a sling and a bandage round his head. There was
also a girl from Kaladia refugee camp. She bore no trace of
beatings on her body.

My client Isam was among them. I had been allowed only
one visit to him before the trial, but had arrived ten minutes late
and the visit had been cancelled.

They were tried before a juvenile court. I had volunteered
to defend them. The prosecutor refused to postpone the trial till
I could attend, as she (the prosecutor) was pregnant.

"Doesn't it bother you to see these children dragged into
court ?"

"I see nothing wrong with it," she replied.

The charges were read in Hebrew. The children did not
understand a word. The police said, "We have to finish with them
today."

In one corner I saw a child with glasses. At a student
demonstration, the Israeli television had taken his picture and
asked him a question. In answering, he had declared his support
for the demonstration.

I went to him, but the police prevented me from speaking
to him. "After showing him on television to brag about your
democracy, you arrest him," I say to the police. "There is no
connection between the two events," they say.

The injured child described how the police 'took care' of
him, but the prosecution witness claimed he was hurt by stones
thrown at him by his friends. "What about his broken hand ?"
I asked. "I think it was also done by a stone." "But you saw them
beating me," shouted the child.

The prosecution witness insisted on his denial. The
court adjourned. The children swapped stories about life in prison.

In the eyes of these young people one could see that they too stood firm against the occupation.

THE CAMP

It was sunny as we visited the refugee camp at the village of Jabalia in Gaza. The mud was almost dry. Old people were sitting at the doors of thei r huts enjoying the sunshine which rarely entered their houses.

My companions represented two generations of refugees. Sitting in the camp post, there was before us a large stretch of empty land. They told me that the so-called 'security road' ran through it, built by the Israeli army in 1971. Twenty thousand refugees used to live there, but were forced to leave the area. They were moved to Khan Yunis and the West Bank. Some of them left the area completely. At one time the camp in this area was called the 'Palestinian's Vietnam'. By day it was controlled by the Israeli army, and by night by the Fedayeen. We could see a pool of water at the side of the road. It was called al-Rashidia but the people used to call it 'death water'. At that time, in curfew hours, refugees were ordered to stand long hours in the pool, guarded by soldiers.

"Here was my first house in the camp, demolished for the security road." Nearby was a tent of rags and a hut built of tin sheets. "A woman lives here with her children. They demolished her house a long time ago, when they found a bunker underneath it. She was forbidden to build on the same site."

We continued our tour by car. "This is my second house, or rather, its ruins. The one they are destroying now is in fact my

third. The first house, from which I was driven in 1948 is a
demolished house as far as I am concerned."

We reach an area where the mud is dry.There are
groups of children in school uniform waiting for their shift to
go in to school, which has neither courtyard nor playground.
The only place to wait is the road.

We arrive at the tent of my companion, Said Ghanim.
It was donated by the Red Cross. Its floor was concrete. Until
November there had been a house on the site, which now houses
Said, his wife, father, grandmother and brothers. He cleared
the ruins of the house to make room for the tent. Everything
they owned was in it. "I'm glad the concrete floor was left,"
commented Said. His brother Hashim had been arrested and
accused of being a member of a Palestinian organization, and
the house had been demolished without prior notice. The soldiers
had come with a tractor, but couldn't get it up the narrow lanes
between the houses, so they had done the job with their axes.
The children had watched silently. The demolition of a house
was no longer an unusual scene for children brought up among
ruins. They were the third generation of refugees.

My companion continued, "Almost every night military
government officials came to check that we hadn't rebuilt a
single room. Anyone whose house had been demolished was
forbidden to rebuild." The hardships must remain harsh.

WITH BLOOD AND TEARS

Palestinian women in the occupied territories are bringing up a
third generation of refugees. That new generation does not know
the whole story, and were not there when it began, but they are

still struggling for freedom. They have been taught the colours
of the Palestinian flag, and have been named Falestine(Palestine)
Nidal (struggle), Asifa (storm), and Thawra (revolution).

The Arab women, whether behind bars or living in the
'big prison', as Palestinians call life under the occupation, have
preserved their honour and dignity.

When peace comes, we will read the history of their
struggle, and find it written in blood and tears.

THE EYES

It was the first time it had ever happened to me: to meet someone
in the morning and fail to recognise him in the evening. It was a
pale, blank face with two bleeding eyes which seemed about to
explode.

His name was Jamil Abu Garbiya, released from prison
the day before I met him. He was sitting with his mother, who
was gazing at him, his face and eyes, talking to herself all the
while. She was thanking God for keeping her son alive, perhaps.

He had been arrested a few days before, after the siege
of al-Aqsa mosque, accused of demonstrating and writing a leaf-
let. When he refused to confess, he was stripped and forced to
sit in a pool of water, then beaten all over, "on all my organs,"
as he shyly put it. He was still a boy. I wondered how his body
had not been destroyed. "At first," he said, "they beat me until
I couldn't see. I felt the blood covering my eyes and the pain all
over, and I couldn't stand. My friends thought I would die. I
wasn't given any first aid. They were afraid to release me like
that. It was strange to see them give me a mirror."

The bleeding eyes looked at me. They scared me, and Jamil understands, covering them with sunglasses. "My eyes are better today", he says, "they were swollen before." Then he showed me his other bruises all over his body. "Thank God he was not blinded," says his mother.

NABLUS REVOLTS

"The children are in action," says a man as he watches a small boy carrying a stone nearly as big as himself. His friends do the same. One stone after another, and the road is blocked.

The military governor was surprised at the blockades.. "How did this happen ?" Obeying strict orders, soldiers forced their way into the school yard and attacked the pupils with clubs. Nearby, Jewish settlers were building permanent homes in Kaddum. The occupation was entering its ninth year, but the people were determined to continue the strike. They had little to eat, but were ready for hunger.

The military governor was worried. He had ordered his men to round up everyone suspected of inciting the revolt, and sworn to bring them to trial. He would order the punishments to be harsh: the judges would oblige in helping to 'protect the public'.

He received a strange report. His men had failed to find any troublemakers. The bakers, pharmacists, shoemakers and shopkeepers all stayed at home, as if striken by the plague. Thus they closed the city, so that if punishment came, it would be for everyone.

It was up to the military government to prove their presence and strength, as they had done before with tanks, machine guns and steel-helmeted soldiers to patrol the streets.

Suddenly, I saw a soldier raise a hand to strike, using the other to protect himself. My companion said, "A number of the injured were taken to hospital."

I gazed at the soldiers, trying in vain to read something in their eyes. A group of young people were standing at a corner. An old man passed and gave the soldiers a hard look. The silence of the iron doors was a challenge speaking in a thousand languages.

THE MOTHERS

They dragged him away like a rag, humiliating your son. They wore red helmets, and carried clubs and guns in their hands. In yours was a loaf and a glass of water. They took him while he was eating.

They beat him as you watched till he fell motionless. You shouted "God is greater". They took him away to a car. In Hebron, near the Tomb of the Patriarchs, they threw him on the ground. You wept, touched his beaten body, and put water on his face. A woman came out of a nearby restaurant for the Jewish settlers and said, when she saw me, "Don't worry, they will always weep and wail."

Your son and others were thrown on the ground there. I asked permission to help him recover. We managed to rescue him from them and take him to hospital. There he came round.

The doctors were astonished. "How did you do it ? Even the doctors were beaten when they tried to give help." One doctor added, "The mothers have succeeded where we failed."

JERUSALEM

Jerusalem is very stubborn. She learns no lessons from the past,
does not understand the language of confiscation and bulldozers
and the cordon of the new Jewish settlements encircling her. She
does not understand the language of club, or tear gas or bayonets,
of shooting and the screams of the wounded.

Today the city looks as if it is occupied anew, as if the
great victory that gave the city to Israel had never happened.
The shopkeepers are on strike today, and soldiers are on the walls
and the roofs of houses, in the streets and everywhere in the
residential areas. They use tear gas, as a reminder of the past.
They examine everyone, checking for possession of that most
modern and effective weapon the occupation could not remove –
the stone.

Experienced officers guard the entrance to the market at
the Damascus Gate.

Things are tense. Everything indicates that the street is
about to explode into a battlefield. The plain clothes police take
pictures, later to be used as evidence of being present at a demonstration, if and when one takes place.

Looking at the people of Arab Jerusalem, it is clear that
even though the city has been occupied, it has not been united. It
will become the city of peace only if its rights are respected.

ANGELS IN WHITE

Muhammad Katamish lies ill in hospital. A prison guard points
to his legs, like the branches of a dead tree, and to his paralysed

right hand. Muhammad looks at us with his one good eye. He was
a construction worker once, but is now too weak to work. He was
ill in Nablus prison for two weeks before he had treatment, and it
has left its mark on him.

He embraces his younger brother, but the jailors order
him out because he has no visiting permit. I ask the jailor to let
him stay, as a humane gesture, as a matter of conscience. He
refuses angrily, "Conscience is my business." The boy leaves.

Muhammad speaks with difficulty. He praises the doctors,
but adds, "They have told me I may be paralysed, but I want to
walk again as I used to. Why did they neglect me ? Why did I de-
serve this ? I have never wronged anyone. Is it forbidden to love
your homeland ?"

I try to calm him, but cannot. I see the nurse looking at
me coldly. A patient nearby screams, "They should all be killed".
At this, a male nurse laughs. Another nurse points at me, "She's
a terrorist like them. Why else should she give them so much
attention ?" But the policeman says, "I'm not interested. You
came here to make trouble."

The nurse with the cold eyes exploded, "He's the danger.
He should be fettered." "Your hatred scares me," I answer.
Other nurses gathered round as she went on. I remembered the
description of them, 'the angels in white'.

Fortunately Muhammad did not understand Hebrew. The
fetters would have made no difference, as he could not move anyway.

It was Israel that had occupied his country, and his legs
could no longer carry him because of what had happened in the
cells of that occupation.

CRY THE BELOVED COUNTRY

Thus Israel Carlibach, chief editor of <u>Maariv</u> ended his talk with
his youngest daughter, published in his paper on 31 December 1954.
He told her of expropriation of land from Arabs in the Galilee area,
and asked her to go with him and see for herself how the authorities
were carrying out the operation.

He told her he wanted her to go, "lest in the future you
tell me in anger, 'Daddy, you did this to them'." But on second
thoughts he did not take her, fearing she would not see what he
saw. "Listen, my darling, and hear our dear country crying.
Stand up, grow, and right the wrong so that the cry will be silenced."

Over the years the injustice continued and increased. The
paper stopped publishing such comments, but the injustice continued
and increased. Our country did not stop crying.

The injustice was challenged, and a general strike called
'The Day of the Land' was declared. The authorities mobilized all
their resources to crush it.

On the Day columns of security forces surprised villages
in Galilee and the Triangle, and a curfew was imposed on them.
In the phrase of officer Malinki, responsible for the Kfar Kasim
massacre, towards violators of the curfew–even those ignorant of
it – "No mercy ..... let God have mercy."

Children, windows, houses and the tyres of ambulances
taking the wounded to hospital, all were shot at. We, who came to
Galilee, saw the holes in the houses. We heard testimonies about
doctors who had violated their professional oath and refused to
give aid to injured Arabs. A young Israeli, shocked at what he had
seen, told us of the torture of the prisoners.

THE DAY OF THE LAND: THE VICTIMS

Khair Muhammad Yasin, of Araba
Raja Hussein Abu Raya, of Sakhnin
Khade Abd al-Kalaila, of Sakhnin
Kadija Showana, of Sakhnin
Musin Usuf Taha, of Kfar Kanna
Rafat Zuheiri, of Nur Shams (killed in Taibe)

They were killed without reason, and there are those among my countrymen who demand an investigation into their deaths. Their young bodies lie in the earth; the land is their identity.

The echoes of the shots were heard in Nablus, Jenin Hebron and Tulkarem. The victims fall from the army's 'warning' shots, and their blood waters the land. Thousands walk in their funerals, bidding them farewell. Against the steel helmets and the shots, their eyes blaze love for the homeland.

Here is the great strength of a giant people. A giant awakes under the skies of the Middle East.